Chronicles of the
Downtrodden

Ken Pennington

ISBN 979-8341074835

© 2024 Ken Pennington

All rights reserved. No part of this publication may be reproduced, distributed, or transmitted in any form or by any means, including photocopying, recording or other electronic or mechanical methods without the prior written permission of the publisher. For permission requests, solicit the author via the address below.

Ken Pennington
761 Sunset Drive
Rising Fawn, GA 30738

Pine Bluff Publishing
Printed in the United States of America

Acknowledgments

I am deeply grateful for the opportunity to share this story with you. It has been a labor of love, and I hope it resonates with your heart as much as it has mine.

I want to acknowledge the incredible work of my good friend Joy Odom, whose expertise and dedication have significantly enhanced the quality of this work. Her meticulous editing skills, insights, and suggestions have helped shape this story into its final form.

I would also like to express my sincere thanks to my dear friend, Russell Hill, for his unwavering support and encouragement throughout this journey. His belief in my writing, his willingness to lend a helping hand, and his formatting and publication of this work have been invaluable. Without his support, this book would not have been possible.

Finally, I would like to thank my wife, Becky, and my family for their unwavering support, patience, and understanding. Their love and encouragement have always been a constant source of strength and inspiration.

Chapter One

Uneasy Passage

From the length of my shadow, I sense I am traveling too late in the day to reach my goal of Craig's Ridge and the home of my friend, Gerty Goforth, before nightfall. I probably left home on time, but as usual, I have dilly-dallied here and there, wasting time instead of traveling. I am walking on an isolated stretch of road called the Scenic and am now passing above the home of the infamous Tisham clan. The Scenic Highway had a glorious beginning. It was originally planned by a few wealthy investors who dreamed of buying and selling cheap mountain land and becoming rich. The idea was abandoned after the puzzling disappearance of two prominent clients. They have yet to be found, and what worries me is that they disappeared on this stretch of road. After that, almost nobody with money wanted to purchase land on the mountain. The grand scheme was abandoned, and the road was left to the care of poor mountain families who did not have either the resources or the desire to maintain it properly.

The Tisham cabin is below me and is obscured by the edging of scrub oaks and pines that partially hide me from their view. I was told that in earlier years, when the house was built, it stood on the edge of an open field of about a dozen acres planted in tobacco, but even then, the house and field were never well-maintained. Now, the fields appear to have shrunk and are almost abandoned, unkempt, and overgrown with patches of high weeds, briers, and pines. Only a small patch of corn is growing there today.

The Tisham boys, all several years older than me, are usually drunk on moonshine and resent anyone passing near their home. They are antagonistic and bullies, especially with young fellows like me. I expect that if I am discovered, they may harm me as they are reported to have done to others. I am tired and desperate from thirst, and I watch with caution as I pass their weathered board shanty, which stands a couple of hundred yards or so down the ridge from my passage. I dare not go there to ask for a sip of their water.

The Tisham family consists of the parents, Wash and Ma, three worthless sons, Edgar, Doyle, and Doolittle, and the elder Tisham's granddaughters, Milly and Molly. Their father, the oldest Tisham boy, was reportedly killed by bootleggers over in Alabama some years back, and their mama ran off soon after with a traveling sewing machine salesman. The girls are about my age, twelve or thirteen, and intermittently attend our school back in Five Corners. Most of us mountain boys consider the girls to be fairly pretty but shy away from them, daring not to approach them because of their uncles.

I don't recall ever having met either Mr. or Mrs. Tisham, but I have seen them on the occasions when I passed by their home. From what I have heard, the elders are harmless enough if left alone. I have seen old Wash, as folks call him, and his wife, too, referred to as Ma. Ma Tisham is often seen in their yard bent over a cauldron of boiling water, stirring their raggedy clothes with a seasoned hickory stick.

Harmless or not, seeing her with her long, frizzy hair falling from a large black bonnet and her long sack dress and apron reminds me of a venomous old witch brewing up some foul potion to cast spells on any unsuspecting passer by like me.

Old Wash, who is undoubtedly in his eighties, has been seen struggling just to hold his plow erect as he tries to till his wretched patch of corn. His old mule appears to be worn out, half-starved, and little more than a walking skeleton, and he struggles mightily to drag that heavy plow through the rocks and roots that are rapidly reclaiming the neglected land. His tillage is littered with stones that have washed down from the ridge, making his plowing hazardous. His no-account sons are of little help to him as he toils, and they don't hesitate to torment the old man with vulgar laughter each time his plow strikes one of the stones and jars his plow from his old, arthritic hands and jolts his poor mule to an abrupt halt.

Bless Wash's heart. He needs to take that plow line to his boys more often than to that old mule. But obviously, he hasn't, and they continue to taunt him mercilessly at each mishap. They are disrespectful to their parents, and I don't like them.

Continuing my journey along the ridge I remain cautious, expecting at any time that the Tisham's dogs will betray my passing. It's unusual that I haven't seen or heard their hounds yet, but fortunately the cover of heavier brush along the roadcut will soon shield me entirely from their view.

Chapter Two

Where Buzzards Soar

I am walking to the home of my childhood friend Gertha Goforth, and I hurry on past the home of the Tisham's with anxiety. I follow the Scenic, but I still have a few miles to go. The Scenic follows the contours of the ridge above their place, and I observe through the boroughs that partially shelter me from their view. I continue to ease along the ridge as discreetly as possible, like a sheep near the lair of hungry wolves.

Usually, when I go to the Goforths, my little brother June Bug accompanies me. He loves to visit there, too, but he is not with me this time, and I wish he were because the threat of the Tishams would be less worrisome if I were not alone. My friend Gertha lives with his mother, sisters, and brothers a short distance from the west brow of Grace Mountain, which overlooks the valley's broad expanse toward the setting sun. It is a place of adventure, and we kids love exploring there.

It is 1929, and I have just turned twelve years old. It may seem odd that I would be so far from home and traveling alone at this age. I guess I follow in the footsteps of my mother. She grew up here on the mountain following six older brothers on excursions, including squirrel hunting, cave exploring, swimming in Bear Creek, and other things girls would not necessarily be doing. I think she is the original Tom

Boy. Now, Mother allows June Bug and me to enjoy the same freedoms she had. She never seems to worry about where we go or how long we are gone. We dearly love our mama, and we know she loves us. Our father is different. He loves us but tries to keep us busy with chores, and if we do not follow his instructions, we can count on a good thrashing when he comes home from work in the evenings. Regardless, we more often choose to take our chances and wander over the mountain as our mama did. June Bug and I think we are two of the luckiest kids alive roaming at will over our beloved mountain.

LAST KNOWN PHOTO OF JUNE BUG
PHOTO CREDIT, ARCHIVE, TRICKUM DAILY

I've heard my uncles talking about how folks are prospering across America, especially in cities like Atlanta, Cincinnati, or Chicago. The country is enjoying something called the Jazz Age, and folks are loving it, at least those living in the big cities. The occasional newspaper making its way to our community of Five Corners reports that citizens across the land are now more successful. They own automobiles, radios, and lots of other new luxuries. Unfortunately, there is a shortage of wealth here on the mountain, and horses and wagons are still the primary means of transportation. I mention this because it is getting late and I am anxious because I have several miles ahead of me, and I don't want to get caught this close to the Tisham's at night alone. I keep watching for a wagon to come along and for the driver to offer me a ride.

My grandmother O'Mally says, not to get too comfortable with all these new developments. There are always thorns in every bouquet of roses. Another of her sayings is that it is best to brace for the mudslide after enjoying the rainbow. We often get too comfortable with our circumstances, and hard times bring us back to a harsh reality. Lately, drifters have been passing over the mountain. Most seem to be good, honest men, but I've heard stories that occasionally mean ones are roaming about, those who are willing to rob or even kill for food or money. I guess times are not so good for them.

Schools are let out for two weeks each fall so we children can help our families harvest crops before winter. Since our family farms less and runs a sawmill more, June Bug and I have the freedom to loafer, so I choose to walk all these miles to visit Gerty. Unfortunately, being an irresponsible youth, I rarely plan well for my trips. When I decide to go somewhere or do something, it is usually on a whim - with no planning at all. I seldom leave home fully prepared for any of my journeys. I usually stuff a couple of baked sweet potatoes in my overall pockets and head out. I depend on obtaining drinking water from creeks and springs that are usually abundant here on the mountain.

A tradition among local folks is to provide a common drinking cup at each spring along the paths. It is usually a glass jar or an empty tin can inverted over a wooden stake at each watering hole. The user removes the vessel, half fills it with water, sloshes it around to remove any debris, tosses the contents to the side, and then refills it for a refreshing drink. The problem is that there has been little to no rain for several weeks now, and most of the smaller creeks and a few springs have dried up. I have walked several miles, and only Bear Creek, which I crossed five or six miles back, had water. The few branches I have crossed since have been bone dry.

My luck seems to be improving. Shortly after passing the home of the Tishams, I arrived at one of the deeper ravines known as Frierson's Hollow. Looking down through the foliage, I can see the reflection from a ribbon of water sparkling in the afternoon sun at its bottom. Descending into the hollow, I find, to my relief, a stream of water flowing from under a small rock ledge. After checking for copperheads or rattlesnakes, I quickly lay prone and ladled the quenching liquid into my mouth. I had half expected to taste the runoff of mash from one of the Tisham boys' moonshine stills that I thought could be hidden somewhere upstream. I tasted none and guessed this was because this water flowed directly from a small spring rippling from under a rocky ledge.

There is an old mountain saying, "If water runs over seven pebbles, it has been purified." I know that isn't true; it's just another superstition, but being thirsty, I don't care. When you're a kid and thirsty enough, you will drink from just about any source. More than once, after drinking from a refreshing brook, rising, and walking a few yards upstream, I have found the carcass of some animal discarded within its flow. Looking a few feet toward the spring, I saw that the water gurgled over a multitude of rocks and pebbles, and that was proof enough for me that this particular branch had been purified. I quickly ladled more handfuls into my mouth and swallowed deeply.

I mentioned my younger brother, June Bug. His real name is Jesse, but most folks just call him June Bug. We live with our parents, Shy and Dorothy Blackspaniel, and our two sisters, Mary Beth and Sallie Ann, up here on Grace Mountain in the community of Five Corners.

June Bug got his nickname from our daddy after he asked him, "Daddy if times get any harder, what will people eat?"

Kidding, our father told him, "Son, if things get any harder, we may have to eat all those June Bugs that are flying about."

Later, our daddy caught Jesse gagging when he placed one of the metallic-looking green beetles into his mouth. After that, our father started calling him June Bug, and it stuck. Soon, almost everyone in our community started using his new nickname, June Bug.

Grace Mountain is a plateau covered with high ridges, stony bluffs, and deep ravines. If not, it usually flows with mountain streams during times of drought. Grace Mountain is a wild, wonderful wilderness. It is mainly inhabited by good Appalachian families, many of whom are my kinfolks. Lately, many flatlanders have arrived, and a few of them are cantankerous, while others are downright mean.

North of the Tishams, there are very few inhabitants, and those that do exist are scattered way back up the hollows far from the thoroughfare. Automobiles along this stretch of the road are few and far between. The road is now so washed out and rutted that almost no one wants to drive their new vehicles over it. Now it is getting late, and the afternoon sun is steadily sinking, so I could surely use a ride if one of those rare occasions occurred. Finally one does come along and offers me a lift. To clear my mind of worry, I find it easier to think of the fun Gertha and I will have after I safely arrive there.

Until a couple of summers ago, Gertha attended our settlement school back in Five Corners. Then, one day, he abruptly quit coming, and I learned later that his father had passed away, and his family chose to move farther north on the mountain to live near his mother's relatives. They live near a stretch of high rock bluffs known as Craig's Ridge. The ridge is slightly higher than any other elevation on the mountain, and it's a place of adventure. It's only a short walk from the Goforth's front porch to the high bluffs where one can stand atop the cliffs and look west out over the valley to the broad expanse of the southern Cumberlands. The distant mountains rise one behind the other and appear to be rolling blue waves washing steadily toward the shore where we stand. Grace Mountain and neighboring Big Grove Mountain are two of the southernmost extensions of the Cumberlands.

I have a small collection of arrowheads that I found under and around those rock bluffs where Gerty and I explore. Most were discovered mixed with the dirt and gravel back under rock overhangs where a man could find shelter if caught in a storm. I have learned that wherever those ancient people found shelter from the elements, they often used them again as camps year after year while hunting for game such as deer, bear, and turkey. While the men hunted, Indian women would gather nuts, roots, and berries and then return to camp to eat, rest, and sleep. I reasoned that if they lost only one or two arrowheads every few years, when multiplied by all those years of camping in the same location, it accounted for the dozens of arrowheads that could be found under just one of the larger overhangs. And that is the main reason Gerty and I love exploring along those high bluffs.

Sometimes, we enjoy a bit of humor when on our excursions. Once, while looking for arrowheads, Gerty and his cousin entered a darkened alcove and happened on a young buzzard. They managed to capture the frightened raptor before it could escape from its perch. At first, it was as though they had captured a majestic eagle. The poor bird flapped its wings desperately in an attempt to flee, but Gerty held it tight. As he lifted it from its nesting cavity without warning, it suddenly regurgitated a crop gorged with rotten flesh. A soup consisting of a multitude of dead carcasses belched out all over Gerty's cousin and himself. As could be expected, both became violently ill themselves and heaved heavily over the bluffs. Neither Gerty nor his cousin ever tried to capture any buzzards after that, and I decided that I would stick to searching for arrowheads.

Continuing my walk towards Craig's Ridge, I am surprised and relieved to see a familiar sight approaching from the opposite direction.

There ahead of me are two of my older cousins, Otis and Bobby Joe, riding on a favorite mare, which I recognize as Beauty. I can make out Beauty long before recognizing my cousins. Coming closer, they stop. Both are noticeably worn, dirty, and exhausted.

"Where are you going, Boogie?" Otis asked.

"I'm headed up to Craig's Ridge to visit my friend, Gerty Goforth," I responded,

Nearly all the neighborhood kids around Five Corners call me Boogie, although my real name is Daniel Blackspaniel. Only the adults call me Daniel. Two aunts insist on calling me Danny, thinking it cute and knowing that it annoys me. I prefer Boogie. I think it is unique, and I have grown quite fond of it.

"Boogie," Otis continued, "It's probably not a good idea right now. It's those crazy Tisham boys. We were hunting in the ridges up there and stumbled on one of their working moonshine stills. They took us hostage and made us work like slaves until the run was cooked off. Four days and nights, they held us at gunpoint. We've had little to eat and less time to rest. Would you believe those clods survived on nothing more than fried cabbage sandwiches?"

"What?" was all I could say.

"Fried cabbage sandwiches, skillet fried in fat, between slices of bread. Those heathens Didn't eat anything else and offered us practically nothing."

"I wondered why I didn't see them around their shack when I passed," I said. "No dogs either,"

"They're still on the ridge moving the still to a new location, afraid we will report it to the revenuers, I reckon. Their dogs are with them, too. They warned them of our approach, and they surrounded us before we could back off to safety."

"Climb up behind Bobby Joe. It's a mighty long walk back home. Beauty won't mind. She's the only one of us that's well-rested, and she won't notice the added weight of your skinny little butt."

Bobby Joe reached down and took me by my forearm and lifted me and I quickly climbed up behind the two of them. I didn't dare to continue toward Gerty's.

The cousins didn't try to hide as I had when we passed back along the ridge above the Tisham's home. If anyone were looking, they could have easily seen us riding three abreast on that big, black horse. Otis and Bobby Joe didn't care who saw us. They were defiant, their anger for the boys was festering, and they were already planning to get revenge when the time came.

"I'd like to bash those mongrels!" Bobby Joe threatened when looking down toward the Tisham's crumbling shanty.

The damage was maddening, and the cousins insisted they would never forgive the Tishams for their brazen behavior. I knew then that they would hold a grudge against Tishams for some time, but little did I know how violent the future would become. Now, while riding on the back of Beauty and headed home, I felt safer, knowing the brothers were still somewhere back in the ridges behind us.

Chapter Three

Coal Mines and Cathead Biscuits

Then, from around a distant curve, there came the sound of an automobile. You could hear the rattling of loose bolts and the squeaking of rusted springs as they chugged steadily toward us. As it came closer, we recognized it to be the roughly-handled truck of old Marmaduke MacKurdy. As luck would have it, he was traveling in the direction of Craig's Ridge and Gerty's. But at this point, I had no intention of trying to hitch a ride. Not with the Tisham boys, all riled up and somewhere up in that direction.

"Wonder what brings Marmaduke to this part of the mountain?" Otis asked.

I wondered, too. He was well known on Big Grove Mountain, where he lived only four or five miles from my Grandpa Blackspaniel. Everyone down near Trickum knew him since he did a lot of business there, but seeing him here on Grace Mountain was a rarity. Even here, most everyone is familiar with him, never forgetting having often seen him driving that old truck. He was famous for overloading his truck and then driving it along the dirt roads at an incredibly slow rate, maybe fifteen or twenty miles per hour. It didn't matter how loud you hollered or honked your horn for him to move out of the way. He just continued on his journey quite oblivious to the mayhem in his wake.

His MacKurdy grandparents immigrated to America in the mid-1800s, and Marmaduke still spoke with a heavy Scottish accent as his parents had. He was known to be quite eccentric, tall, lanky, and perpetually unshaven. His overalls were always clean and neatly pressed, and his long-sleeved white shirt was well-starched and always tucked neatly underneath. It was said he rose at five A.M every morning, kindled his stove, put on a pot of coffee, washed, and dressed. He seemed to always be on the go although, as mentioned, he did go slow.

His old truck chugged past us, with him blowing his horn loudly in an attempt to get Beauty to move out of the road. "Oogah, oogah," the horn bellowed out. A thin cloud of dust boiled up in his wake, but he never slowed or stopped. Beauty, not liking all this commotion bucked slightly and jumped the ditch to the top of the bank, where she turned and waited for Marmaduke to finish his noisy passage.

Riding on Beauty was much easier than walking, at least at first. However, sitting spread-legged on the wide expanse of her broad back soon had my butt and legs aching. I initially tried to ignore the discomfort, shifting from one side to the other. Eventually, my lower extremities became numb, and without thinking I slid from the horse's back to the ground.

"Boys, I've got to walk for a while," I announced.

I had no idea that my legs were fully asleep, and I sprawled headfirst in the dirt and gravel on the roadway. Otis pulled Beauty to a halt, and Bobby Joe dismounted to help me get to my feet. With my legs tingling, the blood slowly returned to my extremities; I stood unsteady for a few minutes, like a rubber-legged sailor on the cresting waves of a tempest storm.

"I guess we should all walk a while," Otis said as he slid from Beauty's back.

A little more than a mile further, we arrived above the McDuffy coal mines. It was getting late now, and the sun was near setting over the western ridges. Mr. McDuffy was my grandmother O'Mally's closest neighbor back in Five Corners, but his mines were here near the crest of the ridge above Bear Creek. The road we traveled passed slightly above the heaps of slag dug from deep within the earth at one of his two most productive shafts. Mr. McDuffy was a good man, hardworking, and there he was, covered in coal dust and streaked with sweat. It seemed to me that there was far too much rock dug from the mine for so little coal, but somehow he managed to earn a living and hold his head high.

Otis tied Beauty off to the side of the road, and we climbed down the bank to where the miner was busy separating coal from slate.

"Hello, boys," he called out.

His blackened face was highlighted by a set of ivory teeth and the white of his deep blue eyes. He wore his customary friendly smile. Mr. McDuffy was a pleasant man and a good Christian. I knew this because I had spent many nights with his younger sons. He had a large family and a small mountain farm. I remembered that on the few occasions when I had stayed the nights with them, he would call his wife and children together at bedtime, read a verse of the Bible, gather in a circle, hold hands, and pray. He mined coal to make extra money to help feed his large family.

We seated ourselves on large boulders he had removed from the mine entrances when blasting the overstory to expose the coal vein. While the cousins ranted about their recent capture and treatment by the Tisham brothers, my attention was drawn to the low ceiling of the mine shaft. How could any man work in such conditions? Mr. McDuffy was a tall man, probably six-five. He listened to the cousins complaints, but it was obvious that he preferred to return to his work of separating coal from shale. He considered the capture and hard labor of Otis and Bobby Joe unfortunate but stumbling on someone's still called for the moonshiners to either silence you or move their still to a safer location. Being held a prisoner and finishing a run was far preferable to the alternative.

"Boys, I wish I had a little food for you," Mr. McDuffy said compassionately, but I ate my last fatback biscuit a couple of hours ago. I'd gladly share if I had any left, but I don't."

The thought of that fatback, thick inside a biscuit set my mouth to salivating.

"When you go off the ridge, stop at your Aunt Minnie's. She should have something to share with you. Tell her I told you to stop by." He turned and busied himself again with his work.

The pangs of hunger gnawed at me now. I had started my journey toward Gerty's with a couple of baked sweet potatoes but had foolishly finished the last of those before reaching the Tisham's residence. Now, hours later, I was growing more and more hungry and was anxious to reach Aunt Minnie's. I even thought I might like one of those cabbage sandwiches.

Aunt Minnie (actually our great-aunt) and Uncle Tom's home stood near the bottom of a steep hollow by the swift mountain stream called Bear Creek. There was little available ground for farming in the hollow, but what was available was fertile, and it provided most of what the family needed. Uncle Tom also worked for Mr. McDuffy and delivered coal from his mines to customers off the mountain near Trickum. His deliveries usually took two days by wagon, but he paid enough to buy the extra things his garden couldn't provide.

Arriving in their front yard, we called out, "Hello. Is anybody home?"

The door opened, and Aunt Minnie and at least five of her barefooted children, all our cousins, crowded around her and clutched at her apron. She knew all of us well. We had spent many a happy hour splashing in a favorite swimming hole just below her home, and her older children often joined us when their chores were complete.

"My goodness," she exclaimed, "What happened to y'all?"

"It's a long story, ma'am," Bobby Joe answered. "But we haven't eaten in a couple of days now and wondered if you could spare anything?"

She studied the cousins and me over the tops of her wire-rimmed glasses while wiping her hands on her apron. "Well, I have just started supper, but that will take a while. I have a few slices of bread and a couple of tomatoes. Will that do?"

"Oh, yes, ma'am, that would do nicely," we said in unison.

She instructed a daughter to fetch the last of her bread and asked one of her sons to run to the garden and pull a couple of ripe tomatoes from the vines.

"But what about your family?" I asked while reaching for the last slice of bread.

"Tom's picking up a couple of fresh loaves as he passes Trickum's store this evening, and I've got catheads in the oven. We'll do fine. You eat this. We will have more when Tom gets home."

Catheads, I thought. Catheads were what mountain folk called large, homemade biscuits. The thought of them coming hot out of the oven made my mouth water even more. The cousins ate like ravenous animals and weren't much better. Aunt Minnie knew that we were half-starved and promptly removed the golden-brown biscuits, sliced them in half, spread fresh blackberry jam across them, and handed each of us a taste of homemade heaven. At that moment, I couldn't remember ever tasting anything more delicious. Refreshed again and after thanking Aunt Minnie, we asked if there were any chores we could help with. After all, she had saved our lives. She smiled and declined our offer, saying that she had way too many kids to have chores waiting to be done. She bade us farewell and sent us on our way.

The road up and out of the hollow was steep, winding, and long. The sun had set and the land was growing dark. Otis and Bobby Joe, having been fed but still exhausted, quickly fell asleep as we rode Beauty out of the hollow. As she carried us up the last ridge toward Five Corners, the gentle rhythm of her steady gait made me drowsy too, and I started to drift off myself. I tried my best to stay awake but was jarred into opening my eyes occasionally when my chin dropped to rest on my chest. I am not aware of how far we all rode while asleep, but I'll never forget our rude awakening.

Gravity eventually pulled me from Beauty, and I awkwardly tumbled sideways from her back. As I fell, without realizing it I grabbed hold of Bobby Joe and pulled him down with me. He instinctively grabbed Otis, and together, the three of us tumbled like dominoes to the rough dirt road.

Stunned, I heard Otis cry out. "Durn y'all, I think I've broken my arm. Bobby Joe, why did you pull me off Beauty? Can't you ride a horse anymore?"

"It wasn't my fault; Boogie pulled me down," Bobby Joe complained.

I said nothing, I couldn't. I had the wind knocked out of me, and a large pump knot was already swelling noticeably on my forehead. The cousin's anger was quickly tempered when seeing the ugly protrusion now extending from my noggin. Beauty paused and stood patiently watching and waiting for us to remount. We didn't, and with my head throbbing, we all decided to walk the last couple of miles to our homes in Five Corners.

Chapter Four

Raid of the Revenuers

It wasn't until a few days afterward that someone reported the Tisham's moonshine operation. My cousins swore it wasn't them, but everyone suspected that it had been. Of all the times for me to finally visit the Tishams in their home, it came the very day the sheriff's deputies made their infamous raid. One of the girls had developed an irritating rash, and although it was thought to be nothing more than measles, they summoned the old country doctor. Since he was unfamiliar with the remote location of their home and since I had suffered from measles a year earlier, I was chosen to serve as his guide. Being in the company of the gentleman doctor did little to lessen my discomfort. When we arrived, we found

TISHAM CABIN

Ma Tisham there with her three boys and her two granddaughters. Old Wash Tisham was out in the woods somewhere, tending to God knows what. The boys stared hard at me, and it was obvious that they intended to make me feel uneasy. I wasn't invited in, but when the doctor entered, I quickly followed feeling less threatened under his watchful eye. I was curious to see how this eccentric mountain family lived. The rooms were dark and smelled of smoke, whiskey, and a soaking of cat urine.

While the doctor spoke to Mrs. Tisham, a pretty young girl peered shyly from the shadows of a bedroom door. I recognized her as Milly, the older of the two Tisham girls who attended our mountain settlement school. Without thinking, I stepped forward to speak. She turned and fled to her bed, half squealing and half giggling. She leaped into a tumbled mass of bedding and flung a coverlet over her self laughing nervously with just her eyes peeking from under the covers at me. She was the patient the doctor had come to treat. Embarrassed at seeing a naked girl for the first time in my life, I returned to the living area, and the doctor disappeared into the dimly lit bedroom.

I heard him telling Mrs. Tisham, "Your granddaughter definitely has measles. Keep her in bed, give her plenty of liquids, and make sure she doesn't have any visitors."

Visitors, I wondered. What are the chances of anyone visiting here?

As the doctor and I prepared to leave and stepped into the yard, we were startled when several deputies suddenly emerged from the woods and quickly surrounded the house. The deputies descended on the Tisham's home like vultures on a ripe hog in a shallow puddle. Not knowing the good guys from the bad, they ordered both the doctor and me back into the house. Old Mr. Tisham wasn't home, thank goodness, only the boys, the girls, and the poor old mother. The deputies had scoured the nearby hollows for their still and, finding none, now demanded to know the whereabouts of the reported moonshine operation.

The boys, of course, denied having knowledge of any of them. A heated argument broke out, and soon deputies were shoving the brothers, and the brothers were shoving deputies. Everyone was shouting obscenities. It wasn't until the mother stepped forward to defend her sons that all hell broke loose. In a loud verbal exchange, Ma Tisham was yelling at one of the deputies, and he hauled off and slapped her. Shocked, the doctor protested loudly at the outrage and was himself pushed hard against the wall. I pressed my slender frame as tight as I could against the wall while considering making a break for the door. I was warned not to move.

Slapping the Tisham boy's ma was one of the dumbest things I had ever witnessed in my life. Guns were retrieved from corners, off the walls and from under mattresses. The ensuing gunfight was deafening-a roaring inferno of blasts from a half dozen deadly, blazing guns. Deputies were ducking, aiming, and shooting wildly while trying to avoid being shot. The brothers were diving behind tables and the pot-bellied stove while the girls crouched low behind their beds. There was yelling, cursing, and deafening blasts from pistols, shotguns, and rifles. In the confines of the living room, the sounds were amplified, and the blasts of guns were ear-splitting. The room was at once filled with thick, choking smoke from gunpowder and everyone was shooting blindly. I felt the doctor slump low against the wall, and I crowded as closely behind him as possible. I could hear labored moaning and heavy breathing.

"Oh God, I am shot!" a deputy cried in desperation.

The ear-splitting blasts from the muzzles of guns left me momentarily deaf except for an eerie ringing in my ears and a thick, acrid smoke burning inside my nostrils. The shooting slowed, except for one final blast. As the hot summer breeze slowly swept the smoke from the shanty, I could finally see through the remaining haze that one of the deputies had made his way outside and was limping past one of the open windows. I watched as a brother brought his rifle up, and as the deputy passed the second window, the brother fired, striking the deputy's arm, spinning him sideways, and knocking him to the ground.

As the noise died down, Ma Tisham and the granddaughters were crying hysterically, scared for each other and the boys. All of us had been traumatized by the sudden and tragic battle. I was sure that the mountain hadn't experienced a fight like that since the Civil War. Then, I heard the low, desperate moans of a dying lawman. He pleaded for someone to pray for him. The Tishams didn't pray, the doctor was momentarily disabled, and I was too young to understand prayer. The deputy died there without God, his shirt was soaked with blood, which was then seeping through the cracks of the filthy floor where he lay. The noise had been deafening, and I could hear little more than the echoes of the blasts ringing in my ears.

But then I heard another voice crying, "Oh God, look at me, I am dying too!"

I found the second deputy lying prostate against a splintered door. He had tried to flee but had failed. With tears washing down his face, he looked up at me and managed to say, "May God have mercy on my pitiful soul!" It was heart-wrenching, and I held his hand until death took him away. In the end, two deputies were killed and another was seriously wounded; a gunshot had broken his arm, but he would surely survive.

The remaining lawmen, those who had waited outside, turned and fled back into the woods, abandoning their embattled comrades. Miraculously, none of the Tishams had been badly hurt except for Doolittle who had the upper part of his left ear shot away. I hadn't noticed until I was helping the doctor into his buggy that the boys were rushing past us, fleeing into the hills in a frantic attempt to escape. As the youngest brother, Doolittle Tisham, ran past me, he paused long enough to look grimly into my eyes, grab my collar, and pull me roughly toward him, and with his face grimaced, he growled, "You tell your sorry-ass cousin, Otis, that we know he gave us up. Tell him he will pay dearly. He's a walking dead man."

It was then I noticed his ear had been cut by a shot and he bled profusely. It reminded me of Grandmother O'Mally's hogs whose ears had been notched by my uncles to identify them as grandmother's property. Doolittle would be easy to identify by his notched ear if he were ever found.

With that, he shoved me roughly into the wheel of the buggy, knocking the breath out of me. I struggled to climb into the buggy and urged the doctor to get his horse to move. I had had enough of the Tishams to last me for a lifetime.

The Tisham boys were considered fugitives now, armed, and considered dangerous. Everyone suspected that they were hiding somewhere in the ridges on the mountain, but several attempts by the sheriff to find them and his posse failed. They had too many cousins helping to hide them. And then there was the controversy. Were the sheriff's deputies even in their right jurisdiction when making the first raid on the Tishams? They lived so close to the county line that no one was sure in which county they lived. Several of the mountain folks differed in their opinions as to which county the Tisham's home actually stood in, and soon, local sentiment seemed to lean in favor of the Tisham's right to defend themselves, especially after the deputy struck their mama.

Constable John Graham Hiram wasn't one of them. Constable Hiram considered the deputy who struck Mrs. Tisham to be a scoundrel who had no place working for the police department, but killing him and the other officer was nothing less than murder. John has worked for the sheriff's department as a full-time deputy for longer than I can remember. His home is here in Five Corners and he patrols not only the county as a whole but especially Grace Mountain, where he was native-born. He is one of us, an honest man who is well respected. John has always worked for the betterment of our community. He attends our local church and serves as a deacon. He never oversteps his legal boundaries and usually doesn't concern himself with minor offenses. But the killing of deputies, especially one he considered a friend, was more than he could tolerate. After the escape of the Tisham boys into the wilds of the mountain, he at once formed a posse for the sole purpose of ferreting out the three accused outlaws and murderers and bringing them to justice.

Cousin Otis, angry with the Tishams and eager to capture them before they could carry out their threat, quickly offered his service as one of the handlers for the tracking dogs. Surprisingly, he requested me to handle another one. I guess it was because we had hunted together and Cousin Bobby Joe was off somewhere visiting relatives. I was reluctant at first, actually intimidated, knowing that the Tishams didn't particularly care for me either. But the fact be known, the intrigue of searching as a member of the posse intrigued me and instilled in me a rare courage. I proudly took my place grasping the leash of one of the eager hounds.

Chapter Five

The White Thang

The Tishams had the advantage over the posse from the beginning. They had grown up on the mountain and knew the many hiding places better than anyone. They had routinely sought out the densest thickets as the best places to conceal their moonshine operations. They were familiar with all the approaches and the best escape routes from each location. Their guard dogs could detect and warn them of any approaching intruder long before anyone could reach their still. But we had dogs too. They were as good as any trackers on the mountain and, with luck, would ferret out the Tishams from any hideout. Our handicap was that most dogs bark loudly when on the trail, so we had to muzzle ours to keep them from warning our quarry of our approach.

Constable Hiram knew with reason that the Tishams would hide themselves in the most inaccessible locations possible to avoid capture and two of the best-known to come to mind were called the Bear's Lair and the Devil's Playground. The Devil's Playground is probably the best of the two locations, secluded and difficult to find even if you are familiar with the area, but it is fifteen to eighteen miles south of where the Tishams fled, and constable Hiram figured they would naturally stay closer to home. The Bear's Lair would surely be the more familiar to the Tishams since it was known that where they regularly hunted possums and coons there. Naturally, Constable Hiram chose to search the Bear's Lair first.

An astonishing natural feature on the mountain is a canyon that has been carved into its western slopes. Over millions of years, the erosion of Bear Creek has carved a deep canyon into the sandstone by the churning action of a relentless tumbling of water. Yes, this was the same creek that Aunt Minnie lived on. The canyon is now hundreds of feet deep and as many hundreds of yards wide. To any visitor looking into the depths, it is a grand spectacle that is both awe-inspiring and intimidating. But with all of its beauty, the gorge provides an infinite number of natural hiding places. Everywhere there are crags and crevices that might provide a myriad of shelters for fugitives. Its upper confines are capped by a tangle of protective pines anywhere a crevasse allows its roots to anchor. Down below, along the banks of the roaring creek, is a dense forest of ancient hemlock, massive in girth and stretching tall in an attempt to reach the sun. Down in the depths, there is a thick canopy of emerald green and the churning action of countless waterfalls and rapids create a constant mist where mountain laurel and rhododendron flourish and help to conceal any potential hiding places.

It is in this rugged canyon that the Bear's Lair lies. It was discovered years ago halfway down a dangerous, nearly vertical canyon wall. Going there requires the visitor to be both brave and agile. You must navigate a narrow and very precarious ledge that normally only animals traverse. Its location is known to a very few of the mountain's more adventurous inhabitants. They hunted there years ago but abandoned their trips after something frightful scared them away.

The lair is a shallow cave formed by a large overhanging rock jutting out from the canyon wall. It was discovered years earlier by none other than old Wash Tisham. It was reported that he and his neighbors stalked and killed a large black bear there. The marauding bear had found the Tisham's livestock easy prey and had killed or maimed three of his scrawny cows. They managed to follow his tracks after a snowstorm and cornered him in the remote den, which has since been referred to as the Bear's Lair. Tracking a bear was one thing, but tracking three killers is another, and I am uneasy. The approach to the den can be easily defended by the outlaws. No matter, Hiram thought it would be a natural hiding place for the notorious Tisham gang, and he was going there first.

Hiram gathered his posse quietly, just at nightfall, planning to slip down the narrow path to the Bear's lair and try to surprise the sleeping outlaws. He reminded us again to muzzle our hounds before we proceeded. Constable Hiram had us wait until midnight to allow the unsuspecting Tishams to fall into a sound, restful sleep. At exactly twelve A. M., he instructed us to lower the flames on our lanterns and carry them with reflectors cast downward to minimize the amount of light shining down into the canyon as we approached the suspected hideout. He ordered us to move forward with the greatest caution. The muzzled dogs strained at their leashes and pulled us along the hazardous path toward the suspected hideout.

It was slow going following the trail used only by wild beasts so the sheriff's men crept along, ducking under and climbing over the debris littering our path. To step off the trail would send a man tumbling down through the laurel and rocks and would surely result in severe injury. We seldom spoke and then only in a whisper. Finally, the lead deputy stopped us abruptly and signaled that we were approaching the suspected hideout. Hiram signaled for the guns to be raised and the lantern wicks to be shone brightly. To everyone's disappointment, there was no one hiding inside the Bear's Lair. There was no sign that anyone had been there in months if not years. We had failed in our mission, and it was obvious that the lawmen were terribly disappointed.

"Dadgum it!" Hiram grumbled. I was sure this was where they were hiding."

Carefully looking around the cave, it was noticed that no human had camped there, but still, there was a feeling that something was not quite right.

Otis and I were allowed to remove the muzzles from the dogs and free them from their leashes. Immediately, my dog lunged forward and headed to a narrow ledge, continuing along the canyon wall and away from the lair.

"What the heck?" Otis blurted out.

"Maybe a coon or possum," I quickly suggested.

Puzzled, Constable Hiram said, "Or it could be the Tishams."

My hound bounded off along the hazardous path in hot pursuit of an unknown quarry. His bark was throaty and full of energy, and the hair on his back fully bristled. His howl gradually faded as he receded around the canyon wall. Otis was visibly concerned for the safety of his hunting dogs, knowing that the Tishams would kill them without hesitation. He desperately chased after his hounds, leading us along the ledge. It was narrow and required navigating over and under thickets of twisted laurel and rhododendron. Surely, any quarry using this path was nothing more than a fox or raccoon.

In the distance, we could hear that the animals were finally at bay.

"Come on, boys." Otis called, "They have whatever it is treed."

Stooping to navigate under the thick growth had us occasionally duck-walking and often crawling along the rocky ledge. Navigating the trail was dangerous and exhausting. I was soon out of breath and sweating profusely. I hurried to keep up with the deputies and our hounds. I was eager to discover what they had cornered.

The excitement of thinking that we might have finally trapped the Tisham boys caused a new rush of adrenaline among the deputies, and we pushed through the brush and rushed forward to capture the fugitives. I jockeyed back and forth for a better vantage point to see past the curtain of tangled limbs, men, and dogs that hampered my view of what waited ahead. The reflections from our lamps cast eerie shadows that played against the deeper recesses of the foliage and created illusions of moving images that were never there.

Suddenly, I heard Otis give a terrifying howl, and everyone in front abruptly halted and then fell backward in confusion. The deputies were stumbling over each other in a wild stampede.

"What? What is it?" I yelled.

No one answered me. All I heard were loud and rude obscenities.

"Run, Boogie, run!" Otis yelled as he pushed past me.

At first, I was stunned, not sure of what was happening. What had been the source of the horror that had panicked all these grown men? I was busy trying not to be trampled and pushed from the ledge, but then I panicked, too, as I glanced back through the thick foliage and caught sight of something moving through the brush. I guess that, with me being the smallest in the posse, I managed to duck under and climb over men and dogs and brush better than anyone. I found myself running past the fastest of them. I didn't have any desire to be eaten alive by whatever creature we had encountered. Finally, we were back at the Bear's Lair, exhausted and desperately trying to catch our breaths, and all were looking back at the ledge from which we had fled.

"What in this world was that?" one of the deputies wondered.

"I think it was a mountain lion," Otis cried.

"But we don't have lions here. There hasn't been a lion reported around here in over fifty years," another deputy insisted.

We sat there wide-eyed and breathing laboriously.

"What about the White Thang?" Another of the deputies asked. "It could have been the White Thang!"

We all sat dumbfounded, thinking of the possibility.

The White Thang, as the backwoods people called it, is a legendary pale-white, cat-like creature that reportedly inhabits the more inaccessible ravines and rugged ridgetops across the mountain. It was first rumored near the beginning of the Civil War. It is said to be nearly white with a large head, long canines, and lion-like features. Sightings are rarely reported anymore, but when they are, they usually cause hysteria among the more superstitious folks living on the mountain. Most continue to fear the legendary monster, and a few old-timers claim to have seen it. As can be expected, no hard evidence other than a random patch of hair removed from a barbed wire fence has been attributed to it. Its existence has never been proven by hunters or science.

"I'm telling y'all, I saw a white mountain lion." Otis insisted. "You can laugh if you want. It was pale white and could have been nothing other than the White Thang."

"Yes, that had to be him," another of the overly excited posse members chimed in. "There's no denying it, that was surely the White Thang."

When Mr. Hiram was asked what he had seen he responded. "I think it was a rather large, light-colored bobcat, nothing more, but then I only caught a glimpse of it since I was almost being trampled."

"No, it was larger than a bobcat," Otis insisted, obviously irritated.

While we considered the possibility, Hiram reminded us that most of the reported sightings had been made by fragile old men while sitting on a porch and whittling on a useless stick; their reputations for honesty were often questionable. Other reports were made by older youths trying to scare the younger children. It is usually those same individuals who swear to have seen hoop snakes, wampus cats, and jump-at-yahs.

Otis insisted that as he approached with his dogs, he came face to face with a ferocious, snarling beast with large, blazing eyes and long, drooling fangs. I was fond of my cousin Otis, but he occasionally embellished his stories to add to the drama of his tall tales. Honestly, I had seen little more than a movement through the brush. It could have been a bobcat, but surely not a lion. Regardless, now that we felt safe, we leaned against the rocks and began to laugh hysterically, embarrassed that we had fled like mice from a hungry bear.

Chapter Six

The Devil's Playground

Constable Hiram allowed his posse to rest for nearly a week after their harrowing experience with the White Thang. It gave their nerves a chance to settle and for the "sighting" to become diluted as different narrators recounted their versions until it was lost in the fabric of the multitudes of other reported sightings over the years.

Finally, reluctant to waste any more time in his search for the Tishams, Hirame turned his attention to the area known as the Devil's Playground. He recruited more deputies and briefed them on the deadly serious nature of their mission of searching out and apprehending the infamous brothers. He again selected Otis and me as his dog handlers. We loaded into two of the county's pick-up trucks and began the long, rough, dusty ride south to our destination.

Constable Hiram carefully briefed the members of the posse. "Boys," he began, "The Giant's Playground is truly a primeval wilderness-remote and particularly hard to access. It is a bizarre outcropping of towering boulders, some three and four stories high. The outcropping extends for almost a mile along the crest of a low ridge, and in the hollow below is another ivy-shrouded mountain stream. Underneath the boulders are several small caves and criss-crossing crevasses. Everywhere there is cover for guarding the approaches to any hideout and plentiful escape routes for the fugitives.

We will need to be extremely careful; I don't want to lose another deputy."

Hiram guided the trucks to within a half mile of the playground before having us pull off the road and park. He was careful to approach the playground quietly to prevent the fugitives from hearing the approaching men and automobiles. This time he divided his posse into two groups and directed them to approach the Giant's Playground with the greatest stealth, reminding his men that the Tishams had already slain two deputies and were known to be armed and dangerous.

He instructed the men in the first group to swing in a long, circling loop and approach the playground from the south to cut off any escape attempt in that direction. He asked his chief deputy to post men in strategic locations there with instructions to capture or kill, if necessary, any Tisham that fled in that direction. Constable Hiram was deadly serious in his attempt to arrest the illusive Tisham gang and bring them to justice. He had the men in the second group wait patiently while the first group got into position.

After a time, he led his remaining posse forward using the greatest caution, hoping to surprise the unsuspecting gang if found. With guns ready and dogs muzzled, we once again moved off through the rocks and brush. Searching through this maze of boulders was hazardous. You could be shot at any time and without warning. I was satisfied to allow the more aggressive members of the posse to push ahead, with me and my dog safely following as backup when needed.

I had never been to the Giant's Playground and found the mile-long outcropping one of the most phenomenal natural areas I had ever seen. Everywhere, there were towering boulders of every shape and description imaginable. Most were huge, larger than the largest barn, and taller than three-story houses. Some were in the shape of giant mushrooms, and others were towering spears reaching toward the sky. Everywhere were cracks and crevices, caves, and alcoves. There were a hundred places to hide and wait in ambush for the approaching posse.

As we continued moving through the maze, the lead deputy finally signaled for us to halt and get down. Ahead of us could be seen a faint glow of light flickering on the walls and ceiling of a cave. Had we finally stumbled upon the Tishams' well-hidden hideout? No visible fire could be seen, but the warm light playing off the rocks above a fire revealed the hide-a-way. Now, the posse moved quickly but cautiously forward with guns at the ready. I was still content to follow on the heels of the posse walking ahead of me.

Once the hideout was thought to have been surrounded, Constable Hiram shouted out, "Boys, we've got you surrounded. Put your hands up and come on out; no one will be hurt."

I heard several loud obscenities shouted from inside the cavern, bumping and rustling, and then the familiar sharp crack of a gun. Was I about to witness another massacre like the one back at Tisham's old homeplace? Pa-zing! A bullet ricocheted off a boulder next to me. Yep, I'm about to witness more killings. I dove for cover. For a moment, it sounded like another horrific battle had begun, but then the shooting suddenly stopped from inside the enclosure. Constable Hiram called for his men to cease firing.

"Boys, give it up and come on out now," he called out. But from inside, there was only an eerie silence.

"Okay, we're gonna toss in a stick of dynamite," the constable threatened.

Still, there was no sound from inside, and true to his threat, I watched as the constable lit a fuse. Until then, I had not seen any dynamite. I watched, slightly horrified, as the trail of fire from a lighted fuse arched over into the cavern entrance. Everyone crouched low behind the protecting rocks, and the explosion rocked the playground. The blast echoed across the mountain, and then everything grew silent for a few minutes. No sound came from inside the hideout. Had the outlaws been blown to bits?

"Reckon we killed em all?" One of the posse questioned.

"Naw, we need to consider them a danger until we can see them dead."

"Ease up that rock and see if you can spot 'em. Be careful, I don't want to lose anyone."

A deputy climbed up slowly, with his gun ready, and cautiously peered into the opening.

"There is no one here," he shouted. "They're gone. Every last one of 'em."

Mr. Hiram's mouth fell open, and then a rage consumed him.

"How in the blazes is that possible?"

Now, other deputies entered the enclosure, still reeking heavily of smoke and the pungent odor of nitroglycerin. They found in the rear a narrow passage leading away through the maze of boulders. The fugitives were gone. Scattered haphazardly throughout the campsite were bed clothing, abandoned cooking utensils, and canned foods. Someone had been keeping the Tishams well-supplied with provisions.

"Boys, there is no sense in pursuing them through this awful maze of rocks. It's too darn dangerous."

I was greatly relieved to hear Constable Hiram call off the search. I was too young to die. The Constable instructed his men to confiscate any useful items they found and to destroy anything remaining. He wanted to completely deny the Tishams any forage or comforts remaining in their campsite.

Then, off to the south of the outcropping, there came the noise. The fugitives had fled into the other half of Hiram's men. We climbed from the cave and began working our way toward the sounds of gunfire. We arrived at the scene several minutes later, just as the last of the gunfire had ceased. Incredibly, only one of the Tisham boys had been captured, and that was after he was shot in the shoulder. Our captive was the oldest, Edgar, and he lay there in the leaves and dirt, writhing in pain, but he would undoubtedly survive. The two remaining boys, Doyle and Doolittle, were nowhere to be found. They had somehow managed to escape the deputies waiting in ambush. They had been able to avoid capture once again.

"No worry, men." the Constable called out. "We've finally caught one of them, and we'll likely catch the others in time."

I had my doubts about that. We had already invested a lot of time and energy and had captured only one of the fugitives. There were still two dangerous men on the loose, and no one had any idea where to search next. We returned to Five Corners with a feeling of frustration. The posse continued toward Trickum with their prisoner and placed the wounded man under guard at the local doctor's office. After recuperating, he would be transferred to our county jail to await grand jury proceedings for murder. At least, that was the plan.

Chapter Seven

Unimaginable Treacheries

The jail at Trickum is a relic that has been surviving since sometime around the late eighteen-eighties. It is a two-story box-like structure made of brick. The jail consists of six cells, a small bedroom for the jailer, and a lavatory for the prisoners on the top floor. The sheriff and his family live on the ground floor, which includes a kitchen where the sheriff's wife prepares meals for the inmates, the jailer, and her family. The sheriff's department consists of the high sheriff, a jailer, and two deputies, one patrolling Grace Mountain and the other Big Grove. In times of emergency, the sheriff can call on several volunteer deputies who make their services available, such as those used by Constable Hiram, to ferret out the Tishams. Most of the time, they work at their regular jobs, such as farming, clerking at the mercantile, or other businesses. While on duty, they usually lounge in the jail's kitchen, drinking free coffee and telling tall tales of their heroic exploits, only occasionally do they rattle merchant's doors to check for illegal entry. Graham Hiram, our deputy, usually patrols Grace Mountain to keep the peace, but he is still deadly serious about finding and capturing the two elusive Tisham fugitives.

No one could have known the extent to which the two remaining Tishams would go to to free their imprisoned brother. No one paid any attention to the dog barking across the street from the jailhouse lawn. His yelps were ignored, drowned out by a steady rain. The streets were deserted, and everyone remained inside to stay dry and cozy. Everyone except the Tishams. The few lights from the dimly lit windows reflected little on the dampness of the grassy lawn but illuminated the darkness just enough for those working mischief in the pouring rain.

The inmate had torn his sheet into thin strips and tied them together to make a rope long enough to reach his two brothers, who waited in the shadows on the lawn. They attached a loaded, doubled-barreled shotgun to the rope, and the prisoner quietly lifted it to his cell window.

It was a little past midnight when a single blast startled the sheriff and his family from a restful sleep. The sheriff bolted upright and out of bed, grabbed his handgun, and began the climb up the stairs when another blast threw him backward, his body tumbling down the stairs, his nightshirt soaked in blood. His poor wife and children had just witnessed the bloody murder of their loved one. Running desperately to the front door to escape into the jail yard, they were met by the two brothers who threatened them but allowed them to run past them to safety. Once again, the Tishams were on the loose and were now more feared and dangerous than ever.

The mountain where I lived was no stranger to violence, and yet those living here still considered it the best of places to grow up. One doesn't so much notice the occasional acts of struggle when seen infrequently. Some exposure to violent people is mostly ignored unless it directly affects them. But still, the bloody murders committed by the ruthless Tisham brothers occupied my thoughts, and it took time for the nightmare of the gun battles to abandon my dreams at night.

Those ghosts that haunted my dreams were fueled by the legends of earlier tragic events that had happened on the mountain. One of the most hideous incidents was down on Bear Creek and just south of the Tisham's domain. There was an account that a mile or so upstream from Aunt Minnie's, there had been a gruesome murder back at the time of the Civil War. It gave me the willies when thinking about it anytime I hunted squirrels in those darkened hollows along that creek. The events leading to the murder were caused by the conflicting loyalties of men dedicated to the Union on one side and the Confederate States on the other. It was said to have happened in the fall of 1864. The story was told that there was a suspicious man who was all too often traveling through the mountain communities with little purpose. When he found men congregating, he would stop, loiter nearby, and listen intently to each conversation. He never joined in any of the discussions and seldom offered any opinions.

Many of the mountain's residents begin whispering that he must surely be a Yankee spy, and having a spy in the midst of rebel sympathizers and bitter Confederate veterans was more than some of the local men would tolerate. Under the guise of friendship, one crafty old veteran who was home convalescing lured the visitor down into the darkened recesses of Bear Creek and into an abandoned log cabin. He was handed a crock of moonshine, and when he turned and lifted the jug to his lips, the soldier raised an axe and split his skull. He was left there, slumped in a pool of his blood, brains and spilled corn liquor leaking from the broken jug. It was said that the assailant, after he had carried out this gruesome murder, quietly fled the mountain and rejoined the army down in Broomtown Valley. Later it was learned that he had a second altercation with two of the victim's associates and was himself brutally murdered. I imagined that Bear Creek Hollow still harbored his ghostly apparition.

It was often told by an old widow who lived in the hollow that she could occasionally hear the woeful moaning of the tortured soul of that slain Yankee and the ghastly laughter of his assailant filtering through the heavy mist that often lay thick on the creek on many cold, and wintry nights. The killings of the deputies by the Tisham boys only added to the realization that desperate men often commit terrible and heinous crimes.

Chapter Eight

Vagrants and Vagabonds

News of the ghastly murders of the sheriff and his jailer shocked the communities of Five Corners and Trickum. It seemed that no one was safe. Most of us here on Grace Mountain were genuinely concerned for Otis and Bobby Joe, remembering that the Tishams had made specific threats against them. I was nervous myself since Doolittle Tisham had made his threat directly to me, and I knew that Otis and Bobby Joe were my cousins. I busied myself with chores and other activities that kept me surrounded by family and friends who could keep me under their watchful eyes. Everyone needed to be careful and report any sightings to John Graham Hiram, who, shortly after the murders of the sheriff and jailer, had been sworn in as the acting sheriff of our county.

Despite such tragic events, life goes on. Farmers return to their fields, sawmillers to the woods, and merchants to their stores. The timber business and the need for crossties proved to be a much-needed distraction for our Blackspaniel family. My father worked hard and kept our family in the woods and out of the limelight as much as possible. He practiced that old adage, "Out of sight; out of mind."

Being born on Grace Mountain has always been a source of pride for me. I was born on my Grandmother O'Mally's day bed in the center of her parlor, and a great-aunt acted as the midwife. The country doctor drove a horse and buggy from over on Big Grove Mountain to deliver me. It was a little more than a two-hour trip both ways. I love our country doctors. Life here on the mountain continues to be much like in the previous century, but now the O'Mally and other farms are changing from the old ways. Split rail fences are gradually giving way to more modern hog wire and strands of barbed wire. Hewn log barns and cribs still stand as monuments to earlier times, but many are being replaced with modern sawed timber. I have heard that you can even buy a kit for a prefab barn from Sears and Roebuck. The horses and buggies of the old days are being used less, and automobiles are seen more often. Still, there are so few cars at night that we boys can lie down in the middle of the highway and take a nap without fear of being run over.

My Grandmother O'Mally is a member of an original pioneer family who came to the mountain in the mid-nineteenth century. Great-great grandpa acquired just over a thousand acres of land here, but that was a long time ago. Unfortunately, the Civil War and other calamities have reduced that holding down to less than a couple hundred acres. My grandmother and my uncles work to maintain a successful farm. Two different cemeteries on the farm contain the remains of my great-grandparents and my great-great-grandparents. I have always been extremely proud that I was born on Grace Mountain. It is part of me, and I am part of it.

I often wonder if growing up on Grace Mountain is different from the experience of any other of the mountains in Georgia, but I like to think that it is. Most of my playmates are cousins, and we enjoy the simple pleasures that life here has provided. In the summer, we spend many hours swimming in our favorite swimming hole, which is located just below Aunt Minnie's house. We ride mules and horses and hunt rabbits and squirrels by day and opossums and raccoons at night. We play baseball with several neighboring communities that have organized teams. We compete in serious contests for championships. The younger children play Dare, Dare a Billy Goat's Hair and Red Rover.

    A favorite ride is the homemade flying jenny. The jenny consists of a tree stump cut about four feet tall, on top of which is bolted a long oak board with a cross-handle attached near each end. Children seat themselves on the ends facing each other. They hold on to the cross handles while a third child pushes the board around and around the stump near the center. This causes the jenny to spin at dizzying speeds, and the children must hold on tight to avoid being slung off. A more foolish and dangerous entertainment is seen when a group of boys gather at night in a freshly plowed field where they choose sides and challenge each other to a clod fight. You can barely see each other in the moonlight as you attempt to pelt each other. Clods of dirt hurt bad enough, but the occasional rock picked up in the dark can cause serious injuries. Often, after someone is being struck by a by a rock a fight breaks out and the game descends into a real hullabaloo. A less dangerous pastime and one that is far more enjoyable is when we all go to Bear Creek and go skinny dipping.

    Another source of entertainment, if one is fortunate enough to have an automobile, is to drive the roads at night while someone with a shotgun rides on a right front fender. The shooter watches for rabbits along the roadside to provide for tomorrow's supper. Once, when I was riding as the shooter, the driver sped the vehicle up, and as I yelled for him to slow down, he deliberately slammed on the brakes, which propelled me through the air and off a steep bank toward the ditch below. I landed without any injury but was furious toward the idiot driver. Thinking he might have killed me, he ran from the vehicle, pleading for me to forgive him.

He yelled, "Boogie, are you okay? Are you hurt?"

I never said a word and lay there as if I were dead. He was in tears as he rolled me over, asking for forgiveness. At that point, I couldn't help but break out with laughter. I intended to teach him a lesson that he would never forget. He never tried that prank again, and I don't remember my cousins ever allowing him to drive on any hunt after that.

My father recently managed to purchase his first pickup truck. It is a used one, a flatbed, but we are as proud as if it were brand-new. It has been a useful addition to our farm, but Dad seldom takes it into the woods. He prefers to continue working our mules there. The truck is mostly used when going to church or off the mountain to Trickum for supplies and the few necessities not available from the rolling store. Mostly, it sits idle. I have asked to drive it, but I am not old enough yet to get my license. Father says petroleum is too expensive and can only be purchased off the mountain in Trickum.

I think Bobo's rolling store is the first truck I ever saw on the mountain. Bobo is our local peddler, and his truck is a modified Model-

T Ford with a boxed-in bed in which he has installed shelves and hooks for the storage and hanging of all manner of hardware, clothes, and groceries. From the back of his truck, he peddles pails of lard, crates of eggs, sides of bacon, bags of beans and peas, bolts of cloth, pots and pans, and a large assortment of Watkins products, including salves, tonics, and ointments.

Most of the mountain folks laugh about Bobo's rolling store. They say that, after bouncing over the ruts coming up the mountain, his eggs are surely scrambled and his milk churned to butter long before he can deliver it to our homes. Truth be told, we eagerly anticipate Bobo's arrival on the third Wednesday of each month, and as he pulls that dented, dust-covered jalopy into our yard and sounds his horn, we spill from our homes with all the enthusiasm of a mama skunk devouring a nest of yellowjacket larvae. All the mountain women are satisfied to shop for most of their monthly necessities with Bobo. It saves them from the long trip off the mountain to the mercantile store, which is pretty much an exhausting experience that usually lasts all day.

When our father drives our truck, mom and our sisters ride in the cab beside our father while my brother June Bug and I are relegated to the back. It is only on days of foul weather that we are allowed to crowd into the seat next to our sisters. On the good days, we ride in the back with our backs pressed against the cab. We think it's fun watching the world go by in reverse. After a few miles, we are so covered with dust that it requires us to take an extra bath and we don't care much for that. June Bug and I have managed to salvage an old, ragged buggy seat to sit on when making longer trips, like to Grandpa's out on Grace

Mountain. The seat doesn't help to keep the dust off, but it sure helps our buttocks to ache less.

Most mountain folks prefer to walk to any destination that is just a short distance from home, like to church, school, or to visit a close neighbor. On short walks, it's not worth harnessing a horse. On longer trips, they still prefer to hitch their horse to a wagon since hay is more available than petrol. My father, being old-fashioned, seems to prefer that method. There are even a couple of diehard families back in the hills that still use two-wheeled carts pulled by oxen and it makes my heart feel good that they enjoy keeping with the old ways, too.

I have been asked how Five Corners got its name. It is simple, really. Probably the best-known landmark in Five Corners is the Methodist Episcopal Church. Just in front of the church, two main roads cross, creating four corners. Later, a third road intersected with the first two, and that created five corners. Five Corners was first established when a group of early settlers built a simple brush harbor as a place of worship. Later the Methodist Church was built there. Soon after, a burying ground was started behind the church, and over the years, it has been filled with dozens of family members and friends. My second great-grandparents were early burials there. Adjacent to the church are two ancient log cabin homes that were built by my ancestors, one of which is still occupied by my Aunt Rosie. The other is now the residence of newcomers that I haven't met yet.

Even though I am young, I still enjoy walking through the old cemeteries. Our community has two large ones and two smaller ones containing less than a dozen graves each. Most of them are marked by simple fieldstones with no inscriptions. I am sad to think we will never know who these old graves contain. I often wonder how long they had been on the mountain before they died and were laid to rest and their identities lost forever. Where did they come from? When did they arrive? What were their lives like and what were the circumstances of their deaths? These are things that I will never know. My Grandmother O'Mally's farm surrounds the Methodist church and its cemetery. My great-grandfather owned much of the land here from the earliest days. I guess he probably knew many of the folks buried in those mysterious graves.

    My father's farm is a mile past from my grandmother's and the church. Life here, until recently, has been good, filled with simple pleasures and no major conflicts or difficulties until lately. We were already poor and hadn't noticed the changes as much as the poor folks who were losing their jobs, their savings, and everything else. The occasional newspaper that finds its way to the mountain is filled with stories of the tough times affecting families throughout the United States. Hundreds upon hundreds of families across the country have been evicted from their homes. Banks have abruptly closed, and people can't withdraw their savings if they are lucky enough to have one. Businesses failed, and the economy crashed. Some people became so distraught that they reportedly committed suicide. Hungry people lined up for a bowl of soup and a piece of bread, and many slept wherever they could find shelter.

    It would have been unusual to see fewer than two or three strangers passing our small farm each month. They would pass slowly, watching our home and, I am sure, considering asking for a handout. Mama felt sorry for them while June Bug and I watched them with suspicion. Most carried a valise or bag with a few articles of clothing. I often watched as they stepped into our garden or field and gathered an ear of corn, dug a potato or two, or picked up a few black walnuts. I watched as they gnawed at a raw vegetable and continued on their way. I guess I felt sorry for them as my mother did. It wasn't uncommon to discover an empty hen's nest or even a couple of missing chickens on some mornings. Men were moving while foraging, desperate to feed themselves, and my father and mother allowed them to gather those small blessings and continue on their journeys unmolested.

  Thanks to the sawmill, our family has managed. We own two horses, a couple of cows, several pigs, chickens, and two strong mules. Daddy usually keeps the mules penned somewhere off in the woods near his timber operations. They are used to snake logs to the wagons or to the sawmill itself. June Bug and I are considered too young to work around the dangers of the sawmill or in the woods felling trees or snaking logs, but Dad still assigns us plenty of work to do. He believes that kids need chores to prepare them for the hard realities of life. At least in my case and June Bug's case, he does. He considers anything other than work as being trifling. Unfortunately, the job he has assigned to me and June Bug had to be the most boring job any kid could have. To keep us busy during the long, sweltering summer days after the corn was planted and the rows hoed, he assigned us the job of grubbing new ground. New ground is any piece of ground recently cleared for a proposed field or pasture. Grubbing consists of digging up all remaining stumps and roots after the initial clearing of the ground of trees and bushes. Digging the roots and stumps of hundreds of small saplings or sprouts is backbreaking. Your hands blister, but most of all, it is boring, especially in the summertime when all the other neighborhood kids boldly stroll past with their swim trunks draped over their shoulders, whistling loudly to get your attention. It was a temptation two young boys simply couldn't resist.

    Our assignments aren't so bad when the weather is cool and the creek water is colder. But during the summer when it is warm, it's a different story. Our mother usually works in the yard hanging freshly washed clothes on the clothesline to dry. She could easily see me and June Bug working through the brush, busy digging at the roots as we grubbed along. As the sun warmed the earth, we would intentionally work our way into the thickest brush, place our mattocks on the ground, and dash off toward Bear Creek to join our friends at the swimming hole. Arriving at our destination, we usually found several neighborhood kids busy diving, swimming, and splashing while some of the braver ones jumped from high ledges into the deep pools and all were having a wonderful time. June Bug and I could make up for our lost time of grubbing by doubling down on our assignment the next day. Daddy would never notice our lack of progress. Yeah, right!

    After a day of swimming with our friends, we would sneak back into the brush, pick up our tools, and resume digging roots as we slowly emerged from the brush, pretending to have been grubbing there all day. Like our mother never suspected what we were doing. Imagine two children working throughout the entire day without requesting food or water, which was pretty much a giveaway. And like our father would never be aware that so little was being accomplished on the project of grubbing acres of new ground.

Both June Bug and I accepted the fact that we would be punished. Knowing our father would either cut a peach switch or remove his razor strop from the peg near the kitchen door, we readied ourselves for a good tanning. We understood that our father loved us but realized that our deception would not go unpunished. We carefully concealed layers of folded newspapers or pages from our Sears and Roebuck catalog inside our pants. Unfortunately, not all of his blows were received directly on our behinds; sometimes, he tanned our legs and arms or whatever we failed to get out of the way.

I was never mean, but I will admit that I was mischievous. I never intentionally hurt anyone, and I never stole from anyone, well, except for that flask of whiskey from Larry Gully's brothers, and I would never have taken it except that I fled for my life from that little creek without realizing I was still clutching tightly to that little bottle. Once, I was falsely accused of stealing a pie from a windowsill, but I did not and felt bad that the cook would not believe me. I was vaguely familiar with the culprit and decided to keep his identity unknown. I was mad that I had been falsely accused. I knew that the thief's situation had deteriorated and he probably hungered for any meal. Besides, there were additional pies cooling in that window.

There was only one time that I was really shaken, or more accurately terrorized, at the prospect of getting a good whipping from my father. For years, we lived in a small, four-room frame house that he built on the property our Grandmother O'Mally had given our mother as part of her inheritance. Father had barely enough money to feed our family, so improvements to our house came only after long delays, and he saved for the next addition. For three or four years, our future living room had a dirt floor that was covered by a bunch of creek rocks. There was no furniture other than a potbellied stove, and somewhere under those rocks was our pet rabbit. Not the domesticated kind, but a cottontail we caught and released in the rocks when it was a small bunny. We provided water, carrots, and lettuce, which would miraculously disappear, so we knew we still had a rabbit living somewhere under those rocks.

I got in trouble after my father finally saved enough cash to cover the floor with concrete. I sure was excited watching him mix, pour, and smooth that fresh cement. After he finished, he instructed the children to stay off it while it cured. He especially warned me knowing that I was more mischievous than the others. After finishing, he got in his truck and drove out of our driveway and down the road. I watched as he disappeared over the hill and then I looked at that fresh concrete. I don't know what came over me, but I went there, walking through his wet concrete. I had barely crossed when I saw him pulling back into the driveway. Somehow he knew. I panicked! Luckily, our home had two doors and as he came in one I ran out the other. I never in my life heard my father curse but he may have this time because he used words I didn't recognize. He yelled and hollered with threats that I was in for the worst beating of my life when he found me. I lay hidden in his field of buckwheat for hours before I dared to come out. The odd thing is, after I finally returned home he must have forgiven me. I never received the thrashing.

Chapter Nine

The Young Adventurers

In 1930, when I turned thirteen, I met Bobby Joe's uncle on his mother's side. He was a celebrated hobo, and when he came home from months of traveling, his tall tales glamorized life on the road. He enjoyed telling of hopping trains, sleeping under trestles, and watching the world speed by as the train rolled across the vast countryside. He even made the hobo camps, or Hoovervilles, seem romantic. I got caught up in his tales and found myself wanting to pack a sack, tie it to a staff, and hit the road. But where would I go? Surely, I thought, anywhere warmer than Five Corners would be better and I was sick and tired of all the senseless killings caused by the treacherous Tishams. Bobby Joe's uncle had recently returned from a trip to Florida and shared stories of palm trees, warm beaches, pure, white sand, and endless views of azure, blue ocean. Without hesitation, I chose Florida. I could find work there, maybe on a banana boat bound for Brazil.

"That's it," I thought. "I'll go to Brazil and live in the jungle." Remember, I am only thirteen years old, but I probably had the imagination of a ten-year-old. Regardless, once again, as was my habit, without any planning, I packed my bag with an extra shirt, a clean pair of overhauls, one pair of socks, and drawers and picked up, of all things, a half bag of Florida oranges. The oranges had been a gift from Bobby Joe's uncle when he came home from a place called Lake City.

I rummaged through our chairs, old couch, and chifforobe and managed to recover a total of forty-five cents, which was good enough because I had planned to live off the land anyway.

I left a brief note for my parents explaining that I would be gone for a while, and then I walked out of our house and hit the road. I hadn't walked far when I ran into my friend, Johnny Smothers.

"Where are you headed Boogie?" he inquired.

"I'm going to Florida. Maybe Brazil. I'm going to find me a job," I smartly stated.

Johnny was fourteen, a year older than me, tall and wiry, and, at the time, my best friend.

"Brazil?" He shouted. "That's the Amazon, nothing but a jungle. Shucks, I'll go with you."

Johnny was crazy like that. It was obvious that we thought like children. But I was glad to have his company since I didn't know anyone in Brazil and would need a friend. We walked the short distance to his home, and I waited while he packed a few articles of clothing, including a new shirt that his stepfather had recently managed to buy for himself. I felt bad that he was taking his stepfather's new shirt. He smiled broadly, grabbed my arm, and ushered me toward the door. I handed him an orange and together, we headed down the road to Brazil, leaving a trail of orange peels along the way.

The next hour, we descended the winding road going off Grace Mountain toward the village of Broomtown to the east of the mountain. We had already eaten two of my oranges. Finally, within a couple of hours, we reached the valley road and turned south. We knew that

Brazil was somewhere in that direction. Eventually, we heard the steady clomp, clomp of a horse approaching from behind, and we turned to see an old negro man riding in a wagon pulled by a large, black mule.

As he pulled up beside us, he said, "Hey there, young fellows. Looks like y'all might need a lift."

We nodded in agreement, climbed up beside him, and thanked him for giving us a ride.

"Yes, sir," I answered. "Getting pretty tired now."

"Where you boys from?" he asked.

"We live up on Grace Mountain in Five Corners."

"Yes sir, I knows Five Corners. I goes up there when hog-killing season comes around. Help most families butcher their hogs, especially the O'Mallys. Y'all knows the O'Mallys?"

"Yes," I said proudly, "That's my grandma's family."

"Where you headed?" he asked.

"Don't rightly know," I said. "Going somewhere to find work."

"Kind of young, ain't you, to be hunting work, I mean. Lots of men prowling around looking for work these days."

We didn't answer, and I thought of the "men prowling" part of his statement. It made me uncomfortable. He didn't ask us anything else; we just rode along in silence, bouncing from rut to rut.

"Want an orange? I asked while lifting the bag toward him.

"An orange, yes, thank you, I'd surely like one. Be mighty good about now," he said, reaching in and removing one of our last oranges.

We had traveled one day and nearly twenty-five miles, and our orange snacks were already nearly depleted. Finally, he pulled his mule to a halt and pointed to the road he was taking to his home.

"Well, boys," he said, "Here is where I turn off. I thanks you for the orange and wish you the best in your travels, and I hopes you find work."

He reached into a bag behind him and removed a small sack. "Here, take this. It's beef jerky. I always keep a sack with me anytime I'm making deliveries. It should keep you going for a while, I reckon."

We were more than delighted with his life-saving gift. As he continued down the lane, we were already gnawing at strips of jerky. It was getting late, and we were looking for a warm place to rest and sleep for the night. We came to a sign that said Broomtown, one mile. Broomtown was a small town with several stores, and it had sidewalks and even gas lamps lighting its main street. We felt safe and comfortable here. At the back of a café, we noticed a small group of men waiting at the rear door. Asking, we were told that at the end of the day, they sometimes shared leftovers with passing hobos. Johnny and I immediately fell into line.

The fare that night was warm beef stew and a piece of cornbread, and it couldn't have come at a better time. We ate with the other hobos and enjoyed the many stories they shared of their travels. After eating our stew, we were invited to join them for the night under one of the railroad overpasses. Johnny climbed into a ditch and recovered a tattered piece of tarpaulin, which we hoped would help keep us reasonably warm during the night. No fire was built; the hobos said it could attract the attention of hostile lawmen who too often tore up camps and ran off or arrested unwanted vagabonds. The evening was cool, and a brisk breeze blew the cold air under and around our piece of torn canvas. I could never get comfortable and shivered through most of a miserable night.

As I woke from a less-than-restful sleep, the eastern sky was just beginning to glow a greyish pink. We found most of the hobos already gone. We guessed they were either too cold to sleep or were already beginning a day of scavenging for food. I was glad we were traveling to the warmer climes of Florida. With our hosts gone, we removed the sack the old negro gentleman had shared with us, and with our teeth, we tore bits of jerky for our breakfast.

By late afternoon, Broomtown was miles behind us. The road we chose to travel south was US 27, and a road sign with a directional arrow said, "Columbus, 82 miles." At least we were on the right road and headed south toward the Florida panhandle. Saving our jerky, we ate our last two oranges. No worries, we thought, we still had forty-five cents for any emergency.

Later in the day, as the evening sun was setting, we were tired and growing hungry again. We still had the last strips of jerky, but we held onto that as our last defense against starvation. The country we traveled through was mostly wooded hills interspersed with a patchwork of farms that were dominated by large and impressive country houses matched with equally large barns and other outbuildings.

Johnny pointed to one of the barns and said, "Boogie, let's check out this barn. I bet its loft is filled with piles of soft hay. It would make a nice, warm bed for us tonight."

The evening sun was setting, and its last rays showered the landscape with a warm glow. An inviting, softer shower of pale yellow filtered through the embroidered curtains in each of those cozy farmhouse windows, causing a sad tightening in my chest. I imagined a father resting in his favorite chair, reading the pages of the local newspaper. The mother was at the kitchen sink washing the last of the dishes used to serve a wonderful country supper. The children were in the living room on their knees playing with their favorite toys. I tried hard not to get homesick. We were so far from home and Brazil, our ultimate goal, was still miles away.

We left the road where we traveled, walked to the pasture fence, and stood watching to be sure no one was going to see us sneak into the barn. With the coast clear we climbed the fence, careful to avoid the top strand of barbed wire, and ran for the cover of the night's shelter. In the hallway, we found several other inhabitants gathering for the night: Cows, a couple of mules, and several chickens heading for their roost in the upper rafters. Johnny and I eased along, careful not to disturb the resident animals, and climbed the ladder into the loft. As was their habit, the chickens cackled and squawked loudly as they flew up into the loft to roost on the upper rafters. The noise, a customary part of farm life, attracted no one.

Johnny and I barely whispered as we climbed the ladder into the loft and nestled deep into the hay for warmth. It had a pleasant smell, and I again felt a tinge of homesickness, being reminded of Grandmother O'Mally's barn and the hay I had helped to store there. Johnny and I both slept soundly through the night, warm and toasty. Just before dawn, we were awakened by the soft voice of the farmer as he was speaking to his cows.

"Morning, Half Pint," I heard him say.

I reached through the hay and shook Johnny's leg.

"Listen," I said. "The farmer is down in a stall milking his cows."

Johnny raised slightly, resting on his elbow. "Shee," he whispered.

We listened as the farmer talked to his cows as if they were his children. "Did you have a good night, Half Pint? How about you, Bossy?"

I almost laughed out loud, and then a sickening feeling came over me.

Whispering to Johnny, I wondered aloud, "What if the farmer were to climb into the loft with his pitchfork to toss down some of this hay for his cows."

The idea of being impaled on the end of a pitchfork terrified me. We lay there hidden under his hay, frantic as to what we would do if he came into the loft with his pitchfork. Finally, we heard him pick up his milk pail, remove his milking stool, open the stall door, and drive his cows out into the pasture. We could hear his voice receding as he continued to talk to his farm animals while walking back toward his home.

I felt perspiration collecting on my brow. We waited quietly for a few minutes before daring to climb down from the loft and ease out the door. We looked carefully to make sure all was clear. Then Johnny spotted a hen's nest with a few eggs in one of the nesting boxes along the wall. He quickly gathered four and slid them into his overall pockets. Exiting the barn door, we started in a quick sprint for the highway toward Columbus. Startled by our sudden dash to get away, the chickens scattered in a wild display of cackling. The farmer's dogs were alerted to our presence and began barking aggressively. The farmer, seeing us running from his barn, ran back into his house and returned with what sounded like a shotgun. The blast caused our adrenaline to accelerate, and we ran hard for the pasture fence. I wasn't as fast as Johnny, and I watched as he half climbed and half tumbled over the top strand of the barbed wire. A second discharge from the farmer's shotgun just as Johnny rolled over the fence caused him to get his dad's new shirt caught in the barbs. It was torn beyond our means to repair, shredded and ruined.

Fearing another shot, I managed to jump over the fence, and together, we ran until well out of the farmer's view. Two of Johnny's eggs had been crushed, and his pocket was soaked with the oozing yellow yolk. He mumbled something ugly, removed the two remaining eggs, and handed one to me. It was covered with the yolk and required wiping on our pants legs to clean. "Breakfast is served," he announced with a sense of accomplishment. He broke the shell and allowed the contents to slide into his hungry mouth and ease down his throat.

I had watched as others had eaten raw eggs but had never cared to try one myself. However, being hungry I reluctantly cracked mine and held its contents over my mouth. It slid in, and I quickly swallowed. Then I swallowed, again and again, three times. It kept coming back up. I was gagging, swallowing, and gagging again. Somehow, I finally swallowed hard and managed to keep it down. My eyes filled with tears as I continued to try and suppress the following gags.

"Whoa! That was nasty!" I protested while wiping the excess liquid off my mouth with my shirt sleeve.

Chapter Ten

People of Dignity

Unlike the folks back at home, it seemed that most of the people living along this stretch of highway owned automobiles, especially farm trucks, and you could hear them approaching from quite a distance. But late in the day, we saw an automobile coming from behind that made extraordinarily little noise. It slowed, pulled beside us, and stopped. Surprisingly, it was occupied by a group of negro youths. Smiling broadly, they offered us a ride. I hesitated; I had never known any black folks except the old man who came to the mountain to help with hog killing. None lived anywhere on Grace Mountain, and I didn't know how to react. I knew that if they had come to the mountain, they would have been treated disrespectfully by folks like the Tishams and I suspected that they had plans to treat us just as badly. One of the young men riding in the back opened his door, stepped out, and invited us to climb into the seat between him and his buddy. Afraid to refuse we reluctantly climbed in. We learned that the car was a brand-new 1929 Plymouth sedan. It was polished to perfection. The youths, two in the front seat and two in the back were dressed in clean and pressed overalls, and they were all in a festive mood.

"Where you fellers going?" they asked.

"We are going to Florida, hoping to find work," we answered.

"Man, that's a long way to travel for work," one of the boys responded.

I sat there in the back seat, pressed against one of the youths, and wondered if they had plans to pull off the road somewhere ahead and beat us silly or possibly worse. To our surprise, they were simply regular boys, no different than me or Johnny. They teased and joked as we rode together through the darkness. In the end, Johnny and I realized that they were not intending us any harm but were simply giving us a ride. I learned a lot about the kindness of people of a different color that day. We eventually found ourselves enjoying their company and laughing wildly as they shared stories of their many shenanigans.

We learned that the beautiful sedan belonged to one of the boys' employers, a white businessman who being fairly wealthy, had taken a train to Detroit and purchased the new car. The young man driving the car was his chauffeur. His boss was now on another business trip and had asked the youth to have his vehicle serviced, washed, and waxed while he was away. His chauffeur did as his boss instructed but then decided to drive his friends to a nearby town with a booming cabaret. We guessed that our lift was a way to share his good fortune and boast of his shiny new ride. After we rode several miles with our hosts, they let us off at the edge of another small town.

The boys bade us a good-natured farewell, and as we prepared to leave, one of them leaned toward me and said, "I don't mean to offend either of you, but you two boys' stinks! Y'all need to find a good creek and give yourselves a hard scrubbing."

Embarrassed, I realized he was right. We had walked for days now without bathing or washing the dust from our clothing. Johnny's cracked eggs had fermented now and we truly stunk. Tomorrow, we said, we will find a pond or creek to clean ourselves in.

It was late when they dropped us off and we noticed there were plenty of sheds and underpasses in town where travelers like us could find shelter for yet another night. The next morning as we left the village, we were pleased to see another road sign. This one said, "Columbus 35 miles." Johnny and I were making good time.

An unexpected discovery along this stretch of highway was the sight of groves of pecan orchards. We had never seen a pecan tree. Here we experienced for the first time having more nuts than we could possibly eat. They were abundant along the road and the ground underneath was littered with unharvested pecans. Back home the most pecans we saw were those included in a small paper sack given to us at church on Christmas Eve. Those wonderful gifts were usually part of an assortment of nuts, an apple, an orange, and pieces of hard candy and we children considered it the best gift ever - at least until the nuts were gone and the fruit was eaten. But here, we had all the pecans we could eat and we gorged ourselves with our backs resting against the tall, shading trees. While relaxing, we were entertained by resident fox squirrels who busied themselves gathering and storing the tasty treats. Even the crows swooped down to crack open and eat the abundant nuts. Finally, after eating our fill we stuffed our pockets with nuts and returned to the road leading to Columbus. Our trip to Brazil was going to be easier than we had imagined.

As we continued our journey we found gardens and fields with scattered potatoes that had been missed when gathered for the market. In other gardens, we found turnips, which we pulled and ate raw. We attempted to bake our potatoes in the coals of our campfires and contented ourselves with eating some half-baked on one side and still raw on the other. Any extra we stuffed into our pockets on top of the pecans. Walking proved to be challenging with our pockets bulging worse than a chipmunk's cheeks.

Later, we found ourselves walking beside a small creek, and remembering the recommendation our black host had given us earlier, we decided to take a bath. We found a clear sunlit pool of warm water with a screen of foliage that sheltered us from the view of passing automobiles. We stripped completely naked, waded in, and vigorously scrubbed ourselves and our clothing. While our clothes dried, we waded, swam, and laughed foolishly while skinny-dipping. Finally, after our clothes had dried, we dressed, gathered our things, and continued our journey toward the city of Columbus. I felt fresh and clean, and I didn't stink, at least for another day or two.

We imagined that within a couple of days more, we would be standing on the white, sandy shores of the Gulf of Mexico and scanning the horizon for Brazil, so we hurried on. A couple of hours later, we arrived on the outskirts of Columbus, a city that was bustling with people on the sidewalks, and its streets were filled with trucks loaded with textiles headed for the market. Columbus was way busier than Centerville back home. It had a river running beside it with a name neither of us could pronounce and we were told that just on the other side was the State of Alabama. Funny we thought, we had traveled nearly two hundred miles, and we were still as close to Alabama as we were back in Five Corners. Columbus was the largest city either of us had ever seen.

Then we noticed a sign that said Camp Benning, twelve miles. Johnny had previously heard stories of Camp Benning and its soldiers. His uncle, the celebrated hobo, had served as a soldier there, achieving the rank of corporal. He later glamorized military life at Camp Benning. Now, here we were near the military camp which was surely full of tanks, cannons, and soldiers. Wow! We had not thought of seeing an army camp. Being adolescents, our goals were momentarily set aside. Now we were thinking of going there, visiting with the soldiers, and seeing tanks, cannons, and airplanes. Johnny and I were much too young to join the military, but we thought that visiting with them for a few days might be fun.

"It's not that far so why not go there and see them?" Johnny suggested.

So we changed our direction and were headed southeast a few miles to explore Camp Benning. Arriving there we were disappointed to see very few of the army's personnel. Men in uniform stood at the gates and prevented us from entering. We stood by the roadside, disappointed that we were not allowed to explore the camp and see its soldiers.

Then our attention returned to our goal of Brazil. There, we would be able to explore where we pleased. It would be fun living in the Amazon jungle with nobody telling us what we could do. The

Amazon, we thought, would probably be similar to Georgia's Okefenokee Swamp about which we had often heard. Now our adolescent minds began considering thoughts of exploring the Okefenokee. We soon found ourselves discussing the possibility of going there first and familiarizing ourselves with its jungle-like environment. We knew that it had lots of alligators just as the Amazon would have. Yes, we thought, we should go there first so we would know what to expect when we reached our goal of Brazil.

The fact that we were changing our direction and planning to traverse the entire width of South Georgia to get to the swamp didn't bother us. We had no real agenda, other than eventually boarding a boat and sailing away to South America. We found new strength in our plan and, without hesitation, headed southeast. We were excited at the opportunity to visit the famous swamp and after that, we would continue to Jacksonville and catch our banana boat from there.

Our hitched rides across South Georgia were few and far between, but those that we did catch carried us for many miles. Finally, we were excited to be on the outskirts of the town of Waycross and near the entrance to our first imagined jungle. Our next ride took us toward the great swamp but was hesitant to let us off when we insisted, "Just drop us here."

"Boys," he said, "The Okefenokee is no place for children. It's full of snakes, gators, and bears. There are even panthers said to be prowling in there."

Being young and ignorant, we were determined to be let out there to go exploring. He stopped and allowed us to exit his car. I guessed because we were becoming annoying and obnoxious. He didn't hesitate and wasted no time in driving away. Standing there and looking into the swamp I was suddenly filled with the same apprehensions I had had years ago when walking near the home of the infamous Tishams. Now caution replaced our youthful eagerness to enter the swamp. Leaving the roadway, we walked a couple of hundred yards through tall marsh grass and finally stood at the edge of a pristine lake. Lily pads floated in collections along the edges of the water creating a pastoral scene. Scattered in the distance were structures of sticks we were sure were beaver lodges. This beautiful scene invited us to wade in to experience our first swamp. As I was stepping forward into the shallows, the water rippled beneath me. I hesitated momentarily, startled at the sudden movement. A fish I reasoned. Then the water stirred more violently, and a dark form rolled to the surface. My eyes widened and I fell backward while trying to comprehend what I was seeing. Then there was a turbulence that was unexpected and frightening. Looking into the water I saw a snake larger than any I had ever before seen. I recognized it immediately as a deadly cotton mouth. Having been raised on Grace Mountain, I was familiar with large rattlesnakes, but this moccasin was truly enormous.

  I watched the serpent float to the surface a third time, and this time, its dark, greasy-looking body was intertwined tightly around another viper. I then realized that they were engaged in the act of mating. I had heard that during this time snakes are even more aggressive. Soon it rolled again and disappeared back into the coffee-colored depths. I stood there mesmerized. I was shaking at my near-death experience. The snake's head was enormous, and its fangs could have completely pierced my skinny ankles. I stood there thinking of the danger. For a moment, then I retreated back toward the roadway, finding my legs almost too weak to carry me.

Walking the roadway near the swamp was intimidating. From thickets of cypress heavily draped with Spanish moss, we heard eerie and unfamiliar calls, squawks, and other spine-tingling sounds. Our last ride had been correct, this was not the place for youthful explorers. As I looked into the snake and alligator-infested waters for the last time I realized that I had lost all desire to leave the safety of the road and wade into the unknown again. There seemed to be little prospect of finding food there and I was reluctant to offer myself as food for whatever hungry critters were waiting in the swamp. The realization that the dense growth of the Amazon would be even more daunting began to set in. But still, the state of Florida, with its white beaches, groves of orange trees, and warm sunshine, beckoned us on. After all those miles of detours from our original route, we were satisfied that the famous swamp was safer if viewed from postcards or at least from the safety of the roadway where we were now walking.

A couple of rides later we found ourselves passing signs for the Florida state line and another welcoming us to Florida. We had reached our first objective but now our desire to continue to South America was somewhat diminished. Another thing was bothering me. Florida wasn't nearly as warm as I had expected for the state known for its sunny beaches. At night, it was downright cold, and finding a warm place to sleep was challenging. Looking for shelter, we first tried to cover ourselves with pieces of cardboard we found lying in a ditch under a large road sign. It wasn't long until the chill forced us from under the cardboard and we looked for a more substantial place to rest for the night. We were on the outskirts of Jacksonville and looking out into a field, we saw a small concrete building standing alone and surrounded by a dense growth of palmettos. It appeared to be a mill of some kind. Finding it empty, the workers having gone for the night, we entered. Neither of us could figure out what kind of business took place there. Metal pipes were running across the floors, up the walls, and across the ceiling. Metal tanks of assorted sizes stood everywhere. Oddly, in one corner of one room, there was a pile of wood shavings into which we hurriedly dug pits which we crawled into to escape the stinging chill of night. We were miserable but also exhausted so we slept in intervals between freezing and seeking warmth by pressing our bodies against each other. We somehow managed to survive the night but I was frequently thinking about the warmth and comfort of home.

The following morning, after brushing off a dusting of shavings and stretching our painful joints, we stuck our thumbs out and continued toward Jacksonville. An old man with a long, grey beard picked us up and asked, "Where are you boys headed?"

"We have traveled for days looking for work but so far found nothing."

We had traveled for days, but that looking for work part was stretching it.

He studied us and asked, "Have you boys been eating? You look kind of frail to me."

"Oh, yes sir. We have had turnips and pecans and lots of other stuff."

He frowned, shook his head, and when he stopped to drop us off, reached into his pockets and handed us three one-dollar bills.

"I'll pray for you youngsters," he said. "You are awfully young to be traveling around the countryside during these times. See that church up ahead? That is my church, and if needed, I'm usually there working. Stop and visit if you are back this way."

You can imagine how excited we were to have those three dollars. Pecans and turnips had proven to be lifesavers but now we craved something more substantial like hamburgers and a cola. Now we backtracked to a roadside café we had passed a mile or so back and were excited that we could afford to order the first restaurant-prepared hamburgers we had ever eaten. We felt like kings sitting there eating burgers and fries while sipping on a Royal Crown Cola. We were going to enjoy our visit to Florida.

Chapter Eleven

Banana Boat to Brazil

Refreshed and with our enthusiasm rekindled, we continued our journey to Brazil. We walked along the busy streets of Jacksonville with the intention of going straight to the docks, where we imagined several banana boats waiting in need of new crew members. Unfortunately, we had no clue which way the docks were, so we stopped a youth on his bicycle as he approached us.

"Can you tell us the way to the shipping docks?" we inquired.

"Sure," he answered, "my papa works on the docks. I am down there almost every day."

"What cha going to the dock for?" he asked in a hooligan-like manner.

"We are going to get jobs on a banana boat and go to Brazil," we answered proudly.

"Brazil! Really? I would like to go to Brazil," he said enthusiastically.

"What is your name?" we asked.

"Name's Butch."

"Papa loads and unloads cargo down on the wharves. I don't remember any boats loading to go to Brazil. Which ship was you planning to get work on?" he inquired.

We were not sure how to answer his question. We imagined there would be lots of boats headed to the coast of South America that would be eager to hire willing crew members.

"I could speak with Papa. He would know if any were shipping out to Brazil."

With our enthusiasm dampened slightly, we walked as Butch rode his bike in circles around us as we moved toward the dock where his papa worked.

Suddenly he stopped, steadied himself on one leg, and said, "You know, it would be much easier to steal a boat."

"Steal a boat!" I protested. "I'm not stealing a boat."

"It's easy" Butch continued. "I steal things all the time. Come on, I'll show you something."

I was hesitant, but Johnny pulled my arm, and we followed Butch into an alley near his home. He leaned his bike against a lamppost and asked us to wait while he disappeared into a lean-to where coal was stored. He returned shortly with something wrapped in an old rag. He unwrapped it and handed Johnny a small pistol.

"I stole this," he said proudly. "Heck, I even stole this bike. It's easy if you are not a preacher's boy."

Back on Grace Mountain some of the most loathsome boys I knew were preacher's sons, but stealing was one of the lesser of their bad habits. Butch arrogantly shoved the gun under his belt.

"Come on," he said. "I know a great boat we can steal."

It occurred to me that Johnny had not yet protested the idea of taking someone else's property.

"Come on Johnny, you're not actually considering stealing, are you?"

"Why not Boogie? It shouldn't be that hard."

"But we agreed to get jobs," I begged.

"Nobody is going to hire us. Didn't you hear what Butch said? No boats are shipping out to Brazil."

Butch hid the bike in an alley and he and Johnny proceeded to the docks where several boats of varied sizes were tied. I reluctantly followed behind and watched as they walked along trying to choose the boat they planned to take. I was ashamed of what we were considering and hid behind some shipping crates. As I watched, Butch suddenly jumped on board a sizable vessel and Johnny hurried to loosen and cast off the ropes securing it to the dock. Now, my anger was festering, and my fear became overwhelming. Johnny had sided with Butch instead of me, his lifelong friend. Then I remembered his stepfather's new shirt. I had failed to consider the first clue.

It appeared they were going to be successful at first but then a large, burly man appeared from a neighboring vessel and, realizing what was happening, jumped aboard the intended prize. Butch was no match for the angry man and a fight ensued. I could hear a lot of loud yelling and crates being knocked over. Butch was kicking and flailing his arms but was being tossed around like a rag doll. Johnny fled as fast as he could run and hid among the shipping crates waiting to be loaded. Then I heard the sickening crack of the gun. Butch shot his assailant. Before he could make his escape, other men rushed him and held him until the cops arrived.

I could hear him yelling, "It was not me. It was those other guys."

My eyes must have been the size of saucers. I slipped from my hiding place and walked as calmly as I could back to the busy street and tried to mingle with other pedestrians. Then I headed home. My desire to go to the Amazon had abruptly ended.

I had no idea what had become of my friend, Johnny. I was angry with him and didn't care at the time that we were no longer traveling together. I walked for several blocks and looked often over my shoulder to see if either Johnny or the police were following me. I wondered if the poor man that fought with Butch had been killed or badly hurt. I knew that at least the cops had the person responsible in custody. The sooner I was out of Jacksonville the better.

My first hitched ride carried me back into Georgia and north away from Jacksonville. I chose the highway toward Atlanta and home. That first night back in Georgia was lonely and the barn where I chose to sleep was void of the soft hay I had hoped for. Instead, it was filled with very unpleasant cornstalks that caused my bones to ache. That night was miserably cold and uncomfortable. I found myself wishing that my old friend Johnny Smothers was with me. Having a thief to share that lonely night with was better than lying there and freezing to death all alone.

The following morning, I was a mess and covered in cornstalks as I walked to the highway and stuck out my thumb. I didn't expect to catch a ride looking like a scarecrow. To my surprise, I was immediately offered a lift by a distinguished-looking gentleman in a large, white sedan. As soon as I entered his car, I noticed his mop of curly white hair which was every bit as white as his car. I was sure that he was someone of importance and authority and yet he didn't object to the fact that I was still covered in tattered bits of stinking corn stalks. He introduced himself and said he was the head of the state game division and was on his way back to Atlanta from Waycross. Since he was a state official, I half expected him to arrest me as a vagrant, but instead, he proved to be the most interesting person I had met on the trip, and we talked about many different things as we rode together. I told him of my plan to go to Brazil but did not mention the events that caused me to change my mind. He told me that he had "run away" from home when he was a teenager and the best decision he ever made was to return home and get his education. He encouraged me to do the same.

Later, asking if I was hungry, he stopped and treated me to lunch. Again, I ordered my favorite, a burger and fries. He ordered the lunch special and as we ate, I sensed that my burger would be the last for a while. There were no restaurants on Grace Mountain. I envisioned an addition to Uncle Tabor's little store with a counter that served homemade burgers and fries. Finally reaching his destination my driver again encouraged me to return home and handed me a five-dollar bill.

"Here, take this," he said. It is still quite a way to Grace Mountain, and possibly it can help to get you safely home. Maybe I'll visit there one day, and I will expect the same courtesies from you."

Attempting to be honorable, I pretended not to want his five dollars, but in actuality, I was as elated as a ten-year-old on Christmas morning. I had never held a five-dollar bill of my own. I felt like I was on top of the world and quickly slipped it into my shoe. I wanted to take no chance of losing it, either to carelessness or to some clever hobo. I took my leave of my generous host just north of the Chattahoochee River in a little community called Big Shanty. I will never forget the kindness or the advice given by that jolly, kind-hearted gentleman who safely delivered me back to North Georgia.

At Big Shanty I found two other men waiting near the railroad tracks to jump any train bound northward. We waited patiently until a train pulled out slowly moving in that direction. Waiting until the passing cars obscured our mad dash, we ran and jumped into a car and found it already occupied by four other drifters. They said nothing and neither did we. They sat huddled together, rocking to the numbing rhythm of the trains clickety-clack while occasionally mumbling something confidential among themselves. My group sat isolated in the opposite corner of the car watching the others with equal suspicion. Toward dark, we noticed a sign that said Dalton. The train slowed and before it stopped, I and one other hobo jumped from our car and ran into the cover of brush. No trains ran west from here toward Grace Mountain. I was on my own again.

Later that evening as darkness claimed the land, I found I was once again passing through Summertown. It was slightly warmer than when Johnny and I had been there approximately a month earlier, and oddly, it was a heck of a lot warmer than Florida. Looking for a safe place to sleep I found a junkyard with an abandoned shell of a truck that seemed a convenient place for a hobo to rest. The seat, although thinned from wear, still provided a comfortable bed. Lying in it was an old, ragged overcoat that provided warmth through the night. Outside, the crickets kept up a pleasant rhythm, which was interrupted occasionally by the distant sound of a dog barking. None of that bothered me as I was tired from the day's travel. I slept as soundly as I had at any time on my recent journey. I was once again near home.

The next morning I was awakened when a man lightly kicked the passenger side door. I bolted upward, with the night's dreams still spilling from my head. I half expected to be pummeled by an unknown assailant. Instead, he introduced himself and was kind enough to invite me into his home to share breakfast with his family. He said I reminded him of his son who was also on the road looking for work. I will never forget the kindness extended to me by that generous gentleman. I was reminded of the warmth of home and it encouraged me to hurry and return to Grace Mountain.

It took me an additional day and night to reach the community of Five Corners. I had been gone for the better part of a month. Before returning home, I stopped in a wooded hollow just below our house and cut a long, thick hickory stick. I knew I deserved to be punished, and my father was one to discipline us children when we deserved it. I had not asked permission to leave nor was I old enough to be going to far-off places like Brazil. Can you imagine the terror of having a child missing for a month and not knowing where they were or what had happened to them? For all they knew I could have been abducted by gypsies and sold into slavery. My actions were inexcusable and called for a harsh punishment.

Approaching the edge of our pasture I saw my dad working out near our barn. I stood trying to summon the courage to face him. Finally, I walked slowly toward him still trying to think of what to say. I was ashamed of what I had done. As I grew closer, he saw me coming across our pasture. He straightened and looked at me with an expression of relief but said nothing. I saw the tears welling in his eyes, but he fought hard not to show emotion. My father never cried, at least never that I was aware of.

I held the hickory toward him and said, "Here Dad, I know I deserve this."

He stood silent, looking at me for a moment, and said, "Take it on to your mother; she will handle this."

He did not ask where I had been. He found it hard to speak. Then looking toward our house he called out, "Dorothy, your prodigal son is home."

Suddenly, the kitchen door burst open, and running out of the house was my poor mother. to my surprise, she was followed by my Granny Blackspaniel from over on Big Grove Mountain. They were followed by my sisters, Mary Beth, and Sally Ann. June Bug was not home; he was off in the woods somewhere. Mama was crying, Granny Blackspaniel was crying, and I felt tears filling my eyes. You cannot imagine my shame. Neither Mama nor Grandmother took the switch. They were happy that I was finally safe at home. After that, I never considered going to Brazil or any other far-away place again.

Chapter Twelve

The Cumberland Crosstie Company

In 1933, I was seventeen years old and pretty much grown up. Most of the families I knew were now caught in the grip of the depression. Few of the small farms on Grace Mountain provided more than the families living on them needed to feed themselves, but somehow they found extra to help their neighbors. We heard stories about the city folks who didn't have gardens, so there was nothing to share. Times were dreadful, and people were starving. My mom's mother, Grandma Blanche O'Mally, was widowed but had inherited a farm of a couple of hundred acres, and my uncles worked hard to help make their farm productive. Being almost grown I worked for grandma hauling hay, hoeing corn, or cleaning cow and horse manure from her barn stalls. She paid me twenty-five cents an hour. The scent of freshly disturbed manure causes my eyes to water and my nostrils to burn, and I often find myself leaning on my mattock and dreaming of a better life.

During this time, newspapers across the country carried stories of devastating droughts and dust storms in places like Oklahoma and the Texas panhandle, which frequently caused the foreclosure and abandonment of hundreds of small farms and businesses there. Throughout these areas people were leaving home and moving across country looking for work and hoping for a new lease on life. One industry that weathered the storm was the ever-expanding railroad lines. The demand for crossties is never-ending and they need a lot of them; hundreds if they can get them.

My father, Shy Blackspaniel, has worked in the woods most of his adult life. When he came of age Grandfather Blackspaniel took him into the woods out on Big Grove Mountain and started teaching him the sawmiller's trade. He began at the lowest position as an off-bearer and worked himself up to top sawyer. Most of my grandpa's family, except for my dad, still live on Big Grove and work at my grandfather's mill. The Blackspaniel family is constantly moving from one location to another, setting up the sawmill and cutting timber from old-growth forests. If the contract is large enough and requires several weeks or months to cut, Grandpa will have a sturdy bunkhouse constructed for the convenience of his crew and a smaller structure built for him and Grandma. Grandma serves as the official cook for Grandpa's crew. The cook's cabin consists of two simple rooms, a large kitchen to serve several hungry men, and a small bedroom for him and Grandma to sleep in. Fifty yards or so to the back of both are the slab privies.

Now that I have come of age, my father feels it is time for me to start earning my way and taking part of the load off him. He figures that if I am old enough to go to Brazil, then surely I am old enough to come to the woods to help him earn a living. Since the days of my foolish adventures, like my trip to South America, I have worked at minimal jobs, like at my Grandmother O'Mally's farm. Now I am expected to buckle down and come to work at the sawmill. He is starting me, as his father did him, as a lowly off-bearer and I plan to work hard and prove that I can handle the job.

The pay is fifteen cents per hour, and I usually spend most of my earnings at Bobo's rolling store when I am lucky enough to catch him. So far, I have purchased a couple of pairs of Dickies overalls and a brand-new pair of brogans. It makes me proud that I am buying my clothing. The funny thing is, I have found that when wearing my new shoes, I deliberately extend my steps to better exhibit them to all the other teenagers.

Even with these contributions, I felt that I was more of a burden to my family than a helpful member. I wanted a better job and with the help of an uncle who clerks at the most productive sawmill in the area, I have found gainful employment. My uncle persuaded his boss to give me a try. I was hired at twenty cents per hour, and let me tell you, I am one proud young man. I am now an employee of the Cumberland Crosstie Company, the largest sawmill around. It is located near the Great Southern Railroad which runs through the valley between Grace and Big Grove Mountains.

My job consists of offloading logs from a seemingly endless procession of trucks and wagons coming from the sawmills on the mountains to the mill. Here, the logs are removed from the transports and dipped into vats of creosote. After they dry, we load them onto railcars to be transported to railroad workers who are forever repairing old or constructing new tracks. My work is exhausting, hot, and dirty, and the smell of creosote burns my nose and eyes as much as all that manure back at my grandma's. However, my check for $13.00 per week is well worth it. After paying fifty cents a day for room and board, I always send a little extra money home to my mother for things she may need. It fills me with pride to think I am helping my family. Best of all, I somehow managed to save a little for myself.

Our sawmill is constantly expanding and stacks of crossties crowd every nook and cranny available. We even have a new sidetrack that was added along the original railroad, and several flat cars are waiting there to be loaded. Our work is dangerously close to a busy railroad crossing where the main highway from Tennessee to Alabama crosses the tracks toward Trickum. I often watch trucks and automobiles approach the crossing, look in both directions, then accelerate across the tracks and hurry toward their destinations. I have also noticed that our stacks of crossties are beginning to hamper the drivers' views of the tracks in both directions.

"I think we should talk to our supervisor about that," I suggested to one of my co-workers.

There were mumblings of agreement among the crew, and I told them I would speak to him later after we finished our shift. Fate is often in charge of one's destiny, and on this day, I failed measurably. It was near the end of our shift and the mill's shrill whistle sounded loudly. Bells were ringing and the saw blade whined as it cut the last tie of the evening. It was then that we noticed a passenger car speeding toward the crossing. At the same time, we were horrified to hear the loud whistle of an approaching passenger train. It sounded out the customary whistles as it rolled toward the crossing. With all the noise of clanging bells, shrill whistles, and the whine of the saw blade the roar of the approaching train went unnoticed.

"Hey, hey, stop! There is a train coming. Stop, stop!" we yelled desperately at the automobile.

The car never slowed. I suppose that all the combined noise from the mill, our yelling, bells clanging, and the whistles screeching drowned out our warnings. We were up on a railcar loading crossties and close enough to see the car's occupants lost in conversation. They drove to the center of the crossing just as the engine of the Great Southern roared through, driven by tens of thousands of pounds of crushing destruction. The automobile exploded! Wheels were thrown into the air to some distant resting place. Bits and pieces of metal were falling in a rain of death all around my co-workers and me. We watched as the unfortunate passengers were carried forward with the train for hundreds of yards down the track. The noise of the crash was deafening with the final screams of the victims quickly fading as death took its toll. The sound of metal, torn and grinding as it was forced along the train's deadly path, was appalling.

GREAT SOUTHERN RAILWAY TRAIN JUST BEFORE STRIKING AUTOMOBILE

Then it grew quiet except for the loud hiss of steam escaping the massive engine and the panicked cries of those of us who had seen the tragic destruction of that hapless automobile. Several of us who were able to run to the stricken vehicle hurried to the aid of its occupants and found, to our horror, five victims: three men and two women. Two of the men were so badly mangled that we knew there was no life left in them. One, obviously the driver, was impaled on the gear shift. An older man who had been a passenger riding in the back with the two ladies was alive, as was one of the ladies. The other lady had been killed when she was thrown from the car and dragged up the railroad tracks.

It seemed to take forever for the first ambulance to arrive and the surviving man and woman were placed together inside. We watched as it sped off toward the nearest hospital in Centerville. The eerie sound of the siren faded as it drove away but then seemed to stop near a bridge that crossed over a small creek about a quarter mile from us. In a few minutes, the siren again reached a high pitch and continued to be heard as it proceeded toward the hospital. A pedestrian later walked to us and informed us that the lady had died there on the bridge. Only the old man still lived and his chances of survival were near to none. We were told that he asked for anyone who could go to Big Grove Mountain and fetch his wife and tell her that if she didn't make it in time, he would see her again in heaven.

It wasn't long until several sheriffs deputies were swarming the scene of the accident and conducting their investigation. As it happened, one of the deputies recognized one of the victims and identified him as a resident of Big Grove Mountain. He told us that one of the family members worked nearby and took room and board in a home just a half mile away. He sent a youth to fetch the family member so he could come and identify the deceased. When he arrived, the scene that unfolded was another of the saddest I had witnessed in my lifetime. The victims were this man's father, brother, sister, and brother and sister-in-law. His elderly father was the only one still surviving and on his way to the hospital.

Chapter Thirteen

Horse Thieves and Hangings

I had been loading crossties for three and a half months prior to that traumatic accident when my boss sent word for me to come to his office. I wondered what, if anything, I had done wrong. I consider myself a good, conscientious worker. Instead of being in trouble, he surprised me by offering me a new job.

"Daniel," he said, "I have a deal for you. We need someone desperately at our sawmill out on Big Grove. Our last man there had a log pulled across him by an infernal, stubborn mule. If you will consider going out there and working, I will increase your wages to thirty cents an hour."

My eyes widened, and surely my smile betrayed my acceptance before I could answer.

"Our sawmill is set in Easy Gap near the horse trail up to Big Grove. We have already made arrangements for you and one other worker to have room and board with a family named Golden there. Your cost will be the same as here, fifty cents per day. They will be expecting you by next Monday evening after your first day of work. Our mill supervisor will give you directions to their home."

I was excited that I would have work on Big Grove. I was vaguely familiar with the location of Easy Gap. It was about ten miles from my Blackspaniel grandparents' home. I would enjoy visiting with them on weekends and maybe going to church with Grandma.

"Since it is Friday, why don't you knock off early and go home and pack any belongings you'll need and plan to meet our foreman, James Dudley, at 7:00 A. M. Monday morning at our mill there? The other worker joining you will be Sam Pinkney, an off-bearer here at Cumberland Crosstie. He will meet you there on Monday." Needless to say, I was pleased with the new offer. Unloading and loading crossties ten hours a day just about killed me, but I was young, strong, and managed to keep pace with the more experienced workers and that had obviously impressed my boss.

I hurried to the boarding house that had been my home for the last few months, settled my account, packed my few belongings, and began the long trek toward Big Grove and Easy Gap. I planned to go to my grandparent's home for the weekend and then leave in the early hours on Monday in time to arrive at the mill by 7:00 A. M. My grandparents would not be expecting me, and there was no way to let them know of my coming. The Cumberland Crosstie Mill had a telegraph, but I knew of no one on Big Grove that had one to receive messages. My arrival would be a surprise.

Steadily, as I climbed the steep wagon road leading to the mountain's summit, by the time I arrived at a point just below the top, it was pitch black. There was no moon to light my way, and I followed the path simply by remaining between the ditch on one side and the steep mountainside on the other. Just before reaching the top I suddenly stepped on something significant lying in the middle of the road.

Whatever, the legs grabbed it me and let out a blood-curdling scream. Then I realized I had stepped squarely on someone lying in the darkness. Scared for my life, I fought desperately to save myself. Whoever he was, he fought just as fiercely as I did. We tumbled around in the dirt and gravel, hitting, biting, yelling, and scared half to death. Finally, realizing that neither of us intended to attack the other deliberately, we slowed and sat breathing hard.

"Who are you?" I asked.

"Name's Pinkney," he responded.

"You're the guy headed out to the Easy Gap sawmill, right?" I asked.

"Yep, and you must be Daniel Blackspaniel?" he laughed. "I walked in the dark until my torch burned out, and I was just too tired to keep going. I laid down right here in the middle of the road instead of off in the grass or leaves where a big rattlesnake might be sleeping."

We sat there, both laughing at our ridiculous scuffle.

I said, "Well since it's so darn dark and I am tired, I guess this is as good a place as any to sleep for the rest of the night. If any rattlers were around, we surely scared them off during our tumbling."

Pinkney found his bag filled with belongings, placed it under his head as a pillow, and together, we stretched out. We were both soon sound asleep.

We woke early the following day and saw that the eastern sky was gray and white with streaks of red against a few wispy clouds. Pinkney heard me stirring and sat scratching his bushy head.

"Durn," he said, "I'm sore from our tussle last night."

"Me too," I said. "Especially where you bit me."

We laughed again, rose, brushed the dust and gravel off our clothes, and walked the short distance to the mountain's summit. It was roughly five miles from the brow of Big Grove to my grandparents' farm. Our paths parted there. Pinkney followed the trail toward our intended job site while I continued toward my grandparents' home. I was thirsty and knew a clear mountain stream crossed the road a few miles further.

On reaching the creek, I was surprised to find my Uncle Ernest Blackspaniel washing a wagonload of turnips and greens in the swiftly flowing water. Ernest was my dad's next youngest brother and the father of two of my favorite Blackspaniel cousins. They were both young ladies close to my age, and I was anxious to see them.

Looking up from his work and seeing me, he said, "Hey Daniel, what brings you to our mountain on a Saturday morning?"

"Got a new job at the sawmill over Easy Gap," I answered. "It doesn't start until Monday, so I thought I'd come out and visit Grandpa and Grandma for the weekend."

"You won't be able to start until Tuesday or Wednesday," Ernest said. "The saw is damaged. I got into a railroad spike that had someone had driven into one of the logs. The sawyers didn't see it until it was too late. Our neighbor, James Dudley, is the foreman over there. He and Papa are good friends and often work together at the sawmills. He asked me to pick up a new circular saw after I deliver this produce to Centerville this evening. Want to tag along? Papa is going too." (Many family members referred to my grandfather as "Papa.")

"Sure, I'd enjoy seeing Centerville and the country over there," I answered.

Uncle Ernest had backed his pair of mules and his wagon load of turnip greens into the swiftly flowing creek where a large flat rock made a perfect place to ford the stream. He would bundle a handful of greens together and vigorously slosh them back and forth, creating a muddy cloud of water that rapidly swept the sand and grit away. He had almost finished by the time I arrived. He carefully placed the last clean turnips and greens in layers for transport to the market. Still thirsty, I waited until the water cleared and bent to my knees to scoop the liquid to my lips.

"Here, use this," Uncle Ernest said, handing me a tin cup he kept inverted over the wagon brake handle.

I stooped, filled the cup, and drank.

"Man, that's some mighty fine water." I bragged while wiping the excess off my chin with my shirt sleeve.

"Better than any water you'll find down in the valley or out on Grace Mountain," Ernest teased.

He removed a piece of tarp from under his wagon seat, and together, we covered the freshly washed turnip greens to keep the dust off them as we rode along the rough mountain road toward Grandpa's. Ernest snapped the reins, and his mules lunged forward and pulled steadily toward home.

When we arrived there, my cousins, recognizing my voice, ran from the house, tickled to see me. I climbed down from the wagon, and we hugged as we excitedly greeted each other. Uncle Ernest didn't unhitch the mules but hung a bucket of oats over their muzzles. While grandma set the table for an early lunch, I hurriedly removed my shirt and washed under my arms, my body, face, and behind my ears. I smelled of sweat and road dust. I combed my hair and hurried to the kitchen table.

Grandpa teased me. "What's the matter, Daniel? Expect to see a pretty gal in town today?"

"No, Grandpa," I replied. "I didn't want Grandma to be hugging a stinker."

Grandma smiled and hugged me again. Everyone laughed. Grandpa waited until I scrubbed before asking God's blessings over our food. After lunch, Uncle Ernest loaded a few other crates of garden vegetables into the wagon and then heaped the wagon high with hay. He said it was a ruse, an attempt to hide our cargo from the eyes of desperate men. Grandpa said it is not the food we transported but any money we receive from our transactions that causes the danger. Men would kill for a bit of money these days, but few, if any, should want our hay. He cautioned me to make friends with no one. The less they knew of our transactions in Centerville the better.

After camouflaging our load, we climbed up into the wagon seat. Grandpa had saddled his mare, and he climbed into the saddle. He was old and riding in a wagon, bouncing from rut to rut often hurt his old bones. I noticed he carried a shotgun strapped to his bedroll.

Uncle Ernest handed me a handgun and said, "It's best to be cautious in times like these." I noticed he had another tucked under his vest.

"You girls help your ma finish hoeing that cotton," he instructed.

"We will, papa," they replied, anxious about our leaving.

Our trip would take us through some rough country. Throughout its history, this area has always been known as the haunt of legendary renegade Indians, notorious murdering outlaws, and the site of brutal treatment of its citizens by roving bands of Confederate home guards, Yankee soldiers, and deserters. Those days had passed, but unfortunately, the area is still a melting pot for desperate and sometimes dangerous drifters hurting from the depression.

The road we followed was genuinely historic. It had originally been an Indian warpath and later became a stagecoach road leading from the settlements of middle Tennessee to Augusta, Georgia. Soldiers from both armies gathered here during the Civil War. The road crossed the swiftly flowing Tennessee River at busy Camac's Ferry, and the Great Southern Railroad ran nearby. Steep inclines and sharp curves slowed the trains as they navigated the mountainous ravines. It was a perfect spot for hopeless men to gather and catch or exit trains, riverboats, or wagon caravans. It was hard to believe when looking out over such a beautiful, pastoral landscape, that dozens of men had literally been bushwhacked and murdered here in years past.

Fortunately, Grandpa had been born here and had kinfolks scattered up and down the mountain coves where we traveled. In his youth, he had had a reputation for being as tough as any man and was said to have carried a half-empty bottle of whiskey in one pocket and a fully loaded pistol in the other. But now, he was a godly man, although he was no stranger to hard times and harder men. He placed his shotgun across his lap and was ready.

It was early afternoon when we approached the small cluster of buildings comprising the Camac's Ferry village. There was a small mercantile store, the area post office that oddly served families living in Alabama, Georgia, and Tennessee communities. There was a busy river port for shipping cotton by boat or train to destinations up and down the river to towns like Knoxville, Memphis, or New Orleans. It was a busy little place with wagons, cars, and trucks parked in front of the stores as others were driven haphazardly up and down the village's main street. Groups of men languished around fires built in barrels, undecided about where to go next.

Grandpa said again, "Boys, remember, do not talk to anyone. It is best to keep our business to ourselves. If anyone asks, we are going to our homes north of the river with this recently harvested hay."

Many starving desperados would gladly rob us of our produce, but Papa had wisely hidden our load under the layer of hay, camouflaging it as if it were nothing more than horse fodder. His ploy worked, and we passed through the tiny hamlet unmolested. It was only eight or nine miles from the ferry to Centerville and the market. We joined several other producers at the farmers market, and since our vegetables were reasonably fresh, the town's merchants soon emptied our wagon. We even sold most of the fresh hay to one of the liveries. The little we kept helped feed our horses and provide a soft place for us to sleep at night. It also helped to conceal the new saw we had hidden under it in the bed of our wagon. Despite the unpredictability of the depressed market, Papa and Ernest still made a reasonable profit from the sale of their produce, which was hidden under the saw.

Uncle Ernest and I seated ourselves back on the wagon seat while Papa mounted his horse, and we began our return trip home. Papa's ruse had worked. Most men ignored us as we passed back through Camac's Ferry in an empty wagon. Some hobos ran to our passing wagon and asked for rides. Uncle Ernest told them we were only going half a mile to our homes, and they immediately returned to their fire barrels.

We planned to travel as far as the mountain's summit and camp for the night at Moore's Spring. The spring was a popular overnight camping spot for travelers returning to the hill after a day in Centerville. It also gave tired horses or oxen a chance to rest. On arriving there, we unhitched the mules and tied them and Papa's horse to a rope tethered between two trees. Ernest fed the animals oats and hay while I gathered dry wood for a fire. Grandpa opened and heated cans of beans, and we had our supper. Later, as we tired, we climbed into the wagon bed and spread our blankets on the remaining layer of hay.

Grandpa groaned slightly and complained, "Boys, this darn wagon bed is harder than Job's tribulation from God."

"Yep, sure is," I said, rolling slightly to relieve the discomfort against my hips. "Guess we should have saved more straw."

"I guess it's better than sleeping down there on the ground with them copperheads," Uncle Ernest said, chuckling.

We all agreed and lay there listening to the resounding in-and-out rhythm of the hordes of newly-hatched cicadas, the chirps of crickets, and the calls of whippoorwills as we drifted off to sleep.

We awakened early the following day to find Papa's horse missing. The mules were standing patiently, still tethered. In the mud around the spring, we found boot tracks that revealed someone had taken Grandpa's horse. He was outraged.

The tracks showed that the horse had walked away in the direction we were traveling, but three men in a wagon had no chance of catching up with the culprit riding Papa's horse.

"Horse thieving is still punishable by hanging out where you live, isn't it, Papa? If not, it should be," I declared angrily.

Grandpa's temper settled slightly, and he grew silent. Uncle Ernest had been busy hitching the mules to the wagon while Papa and I investigated the theft. We all climbed into the wagon, and the mules strained against our weight. We still had miles of steep hills and deep hollows to navigate toward home. The mules had their work cut out for them. We hurried on with little hope of overtaking the horse thief. Our progress was slower than I liked, but we rode along with as much haste as possible. I was still arguing about hanging if we happened to catch the brazen thief. Papa cautioned that we should wait until we found the perpetrator and learned all the facts before we condemned him too harshly. His Christian side was now guiding his emotions.

When we arrived within a couple of miles of Grandpa's farm, we rounded a curve, and there stood his horse, which was hitched to a pine tree beside the road. He was none the worse for wear. A detailed note was pinned to the saddle, saying, "Sorry for taking your mount. I ask for your forgiveness. I am engaged in mining north of Centerville, and while there, I received word that my daughter had fallen gravely ill. After climbing the road from Camac's Ferry, I was desperate to get home and was too exhausted to continue walking. Seeing your horse at Moore's Spring was my only hope. But when I arrived here, I met neighbors who informed me that my precious angel had died of Typhoid. I am leaving your horse and three dollars for your troubles. It is all I have, but I won't need it now, for my life is over. Maybe I can apologize again in the great beyond."

Papa and Uncle Ernest stood silent, saddened at the stranger's confession. Then Papa looked sternly at me over his glasses and said, "Daniel, it is best to wait until you learn all the facts before passing judgment. You still think we should hang the man?"

I said nothing. Ashamed, I looked down and shook my head no.

Chapter Fourteen

Room and Board

When Tuesday morning arrived, I rode with Uncle Ernest to deliver the new saw to the mill at Easy Gap. Sam Pinkney was there waiting and introduced me to the foreman, James Dudley. It was not long until the repairs were all made, and Pinkney and I joined the rest of the crew for our first day of hard work. Mr. Dudley and his crew were well-oiled and efficient. Logs were rolled onto the carriage almost as fast as we could saw them. I sweated like the dickens and Pinkney grinned from ear to ear. He was enjoying watching me sweat. I will never forget that first day of work at the mill. It was hot and exhausting, and at the end of the day, Pinkney and I were worn out and hungry. We walked a couple of miles from the mill to our prearranged place of room and board at the Golden residence.

SAWMILL AT EASY GAP

Arriving there, we found an ancient house of hewn logs that probably dates back to the Civil War. It was empty! The doors of the dogtrot were wide open, and trash had been spilled across the dirty floors. Checking the pantries, we found nothing but dusty and empty jars, mostly lying haphazardly across the shelves. A filthy, corn shuck mattress lay sprawled on the floor. It was obvious that no one had lived here for weeks. Pinkney and I were sickened and disheartened. I prayed for God to rescue us and promised myself that if I could make it through the night, I would return to the comforts of Five Corners and Grace Mountain and never set foot near Easy Gap again.

Not knowing anyone other than my grandparents and Uncle Ernest, who lived too many miles from Easy Gap for a daily commute to the mill, I decided to find a place to camp for the night and prepare to return to my home at Five Corners the following day. Continuing along the road from the mill, Pinkney and I were now walking in the dark, lost and angry. Then, we saw a faint, pale yellow light in the distance. We stumbled in that direction. Arriving at the source of the glow, we found a small farmhouse. The dogs alerted the inhabitants of our approach, and an older man slowly opened the door. He stood holding a coal oil lamp and a double-barreled shotgun in one hand.

"Who goes there?" he called out.

"Sorry, sir. My name is Daniel Blackspaniel, and my friend is Samuel Pinkney. We are employed over at the sawmill in Easy Gap. We were supposed to have room and board back at that cabin down the road, but no one was there. We have worked all day with nothing to eat and now no place to sleep, and we are both pretty exhausted."

"Oh, my goodness." He said. "I am familiar with the mill but don't know who would offer you room and board. No one has lived there for months. The family that lived there up and moved without a word. Bizarre it was."

"Please step inside and let me think." Then, speaking to a woman standing nearby, he said, "Gracie, fix these poor boys something to eat. This is my wife, Gracie, and I am Bill Jenkins. We'll feed you something tonight and see if I can find accommodations tomorrow. You can sleep in the loft up in my barn tonight. Plenty of hay for bedding and Gracie will get you a quilt to cover with."

He led us to his back porch, filling a pan with water, handing us a bar of soap, and invited us to wash up.

"There is a towel hanging on that peg there." He said, "Clean up while Gracie gets your supper ready."

We washed while Mrs. Jenkins warmed over a pot of black-eyed peas and fried some potatoes. Peas, potatoes, and cornbread with a slice of onion washed down with spring-cooled buttermilk, a country favorite, and for Pinkney and me, it was as good as it gets. The Jenkins family had rescued us, and I remembered my earlier prayer asking God to save us. Refreshed, we decided to stay on Grace Mountain and give Mr. Jenkins time to find someone to provide us with room and board. The following morning, Mrs. Jenkins gave us our breakfast and then handed each of us a small, brown paper sack containing two fat-back biscuits and a jug of water for our lunch, and although a bit weary, we agreed to return to our jobs at Easy Gap.

That evening, with the second day of work completed, we walked a couple of miles from the mill to Jenkin's residence again to see if he had found our accommodations. We stared hard at the abandoned home of the Goldens as we passed. Its empty shell now appears to be a haunt for lingering ghosts. On arriving at Mr. Jenkins' residence, he proudly announced that he had found us room and board. He had arranged for us to stay with a sizable family named Burrell. Pinkney and I could not have been more grateful, and after thanking him, we hurried toward the waiting Mama Burrell.

Arriving at the Burrell residence, we found Mrs. Burrell busy setting her large kitchen table with a heart-warming country meal. She greeted us with the warmest welcome and introduced us to her husband and a house full of eager, hungry youths who had been waiting patiently for our arrival so they could eat. Pinkney and I sat for a good, old-fashioned dinner that I thought was as good as any I ever had. They placed a bed for Pinkney and me in one of their outbuildings near a small, bubbling spring. A large iron pot, hidden behind the outbuilding, would serve as our bathing facilities. The water could be heated in the iron pot or left cold, straight from the spring, our choice. Mr. Burrell pointed to a supply of small logs and limbs piled nearby and an axe for chopping firewood.

"You can use that wood for the fire to heat your bath water," he said.

I chose to use water heated in that large cauldron rather than the frigid water straight from the spring, and I immediately went to work chopping wood.

Chapter Fifteen
A Father's Great Sadness

It was a couple of weeks later that we learned that a family named Biddle from over in a neighboring community had lost their twelve-year-old daughter, Charity, to typhoid. Charity was the little girl whose daddy had "borrowed" Grandpa's horse. She had been her father's pride and his greatest joy. He, being devastated, now promised to kill himself rather than live without her. Since he was a miner with access to plenty of dynamite, he swore that he would use a full case of it as his executioner. Grandpa visited with him on a couple of occasions to offer his condolences and plead with him to have faith that better times were ahead.

Weeks passed and Mr. Biddle continued working as if nothing had happened. Every morning, he rose, quietly ate breakfast, hitched his mule to a sled, and went to the mountainside to work on a rock ledge just below the very cemetery where his beloved daughter lay buried. From the layers of rock, he had managed to remove a single, large slab of stone which he intended to use as a cover for his little daughter's grave. He chiseled it to perfection, the slab being about three feet wide, five feet long, and six inches thick. On its surface, he had meticulously engraved a beautiful epitaph describing his devotion to her and his irrepressible sadness at her passing. His family and friends were relieved that he had failed to kill himself. Most everyone in that part of

Big Grove had become acquainted with the story of the Biddle family and the loss of their daughter. Even we workers at the mill at Easy Gap collected an offering to help cover expenses and promised any other help we could give.

A few days after he finished the gravestone, Mr. Biddle's wife visited neighbors near the cemetery when the earth shook, and then a loud boom reverberated across Big Grove Mountain. My father, Sly Blackspaniel, was hoeing his garden out on Grace Mountain fifteen miles away when the tremendous boom startled him. He straightened, leaning on his hoe, and thought, "My Goodness, that sounded like a roll of thunder, but I see no clouds. What in the world could that have been?"

At that exact moment, all the workers at the sawmill felt an unusual quake and hesitated for a moment, looking around for what had startled them. The limbs of the towering trees nearby were swaying back and forth

Mrs. Biddle was sitting on her neighbor's porch talking with her friend when the tremendous blast caused her to bolt upright from her rocking chair.

She shouted, "Oh God, he has done it. He has blown himself to kingdom come just as he said he would."

And indeed, he had. It was determined later that while he searched the layered deposits of sandstone for the perfect slab to cover his beloved daughter's grave, he had discovered a small cave immediately under the bluffs below the cemetery. It provided the perfect setting for his final statement. He "borrowed" a case of dynamite from the mine's powder magazine and carefully placed it inside the alcove. As he had planned, he entered the narrow passage, calmly took a seat atop the explosives, lit the fuse, and blew himself out of existence.

Later, when several of us visited the area around what until then had been a cave, we found bits of burnt clothing, pieces of shoe leather, and shoelaces scattered down the mountainside. That image will haunt me for the rest of my life. Every crack of thunder since brings back images to me of that fateful day.

I visited the cemetery one Sunday afternoon with my Grandfather Blackspaniel. I was at once impressed with the flawless workmanship and the enormous labor required for one man and a mule to cut and move that massive stone up the mountainside and into the cemetery.

Masterfully carved into the stone's surface was the name Charity Biddle, and the imprint of two human hands, one an adult and the other that of a small child. Underneath was the inscription, "Ah, wee lass, place your hand in mine and we will walk together down the path leading to Paradise. At the gates, I will ask for forgiveness, and hopefully, God will allow me to join you there."

It was shortly after that event that a new revival of sorts swept across the mountain, and everywhere, groups of believers were gathering for Sacred Harp singings. My grandmother, already a devout follower, thought it an ideal time to invite me to visit her in her church. Knowing that I had yet to surrender my heart to God, she felt that now was the best opportunity to get me to ask for God's forgiveness for my sins and possibly to become an active member of the church. I loved and respected my grandmother, so I accepted her invitation to visit her favorite place of worship and joined her the following Sunday.

The program started at ten,, and I experienced Sacred Harp singing for the first time! To my surprise, I was caught up in its beautiful harmony and simplicity. I was mesmerized by song after song. I loved how one singer would stand without notice and begin singing a beautiful melody, and then others would join in succession until finally, the whole congregation would be raising their voices to heaven. When they finally called for an adjournment and dinner on the grounds, I realized how much I had enjoyed attending the service with my grandmother. It was then one in the afternoon, and when the singing stopped, I realized that I was starving. Granny proudly escorted me to a long outdoor table piled high with a bounty of old-fashioned country cooking. Granny's favorite preacher gave a long, drawn-out prayer calling sinners to surrender to God's call for our salvation. I was thinking that this was probably the real purpose of my granny's invitation. Then I heard an "Amen." We piled our plates high with fried chicken, green beans, and casseroles of every variety and then moved aside to sit or stand in the shade of giant oaks. By this time, it was generally heard from several gluttons that if we had eaten another bite, we would not have been able to return to our seats in the pews. I imagined my grandmother was hoping that she and the preacher could now persuade me to give up my sinful ways and submit to God's will.

I looked forward to more music but was disappointed when the singers sang only one more hymn. It was time for the preaching, and the pastor enthusiastically moved to the pulpit. I wanted more singing and less preaching, but he was up there now, looking out over the congregation and opening a heavily worn Bible. At this point, I was beginning to feel slightly uncomfortable. This was the part of the service my grandmother had been waiting for. She was sure I would fall on my knees and beg God's forgiveness after listening to her favorite preacher. The sermon started slowly but soon reached a fever pitch.

The preacher was now stomping up and down the aisle, thumping his Bible and shouting as loudly as his voice would allow while trying to get his message across to us sinners. His face was flushed, and the veins in his neck protruded as if they were about to explode. His temples and chin dripped with sweat, and his well-combed hair now dangled like a wet mop, revealing his bald head. Looking over at my grandmother, I could see the overwhelming conviction in her edge-of-the-seat enthusiasm.

I was more concerned with the worry that the preacher might drop dead any moment from a massive stroke before he could preach to me in heaven. Finally, he stood wiping a sea of sweat from his head, brow, and voice, although hoarse, softened. He then pleaded for any sinner to come to the altar. A few rose from their seats and stumbled forward with tears streaming down their faces. Others shouted wildly, lifting their arms toward heaven, all caught up in the Holy Spirit. Those at the altar fell to their knees, and I could hear a loud, mingling of prayers. My grandmother turned and looked at me as I sat there unmoved. She was shocked that the beautiful sermon had left me untouched.

"Well, what did you think of the preaching?" she asked, desperately wishing for a favorable response.

"Granny, I didn't care for it," was my callous answer. "I was afraid he was about to explode." Granny's eyes widened in total disbelief, and she drew a deep, long breath.

"You heathen!" she shouted abruptly, "What is wrong with you?"

All the church grew eerily silent and were looking in my direction.

I loved my Granny Blackspaniel and never meant to disappoint or embarrass her. But I would never have expected her to go off on me the way she did, almost like she had sat on a case of dynamite herself.

Thinking back, I remember that my experience with church and religion had begun years earlier. It happened at our old Methodist Church back on Grace Mountain. I had attended there since my mom took me as an infant. Over the years since, I have never given religion much thought. My interests were mostly the all-day singing and the dinners on the grounds. But being a kid and having little interest in the service itself left me with one other favorite amusement, if not a slightly demonic pleasure, that today bumfuzzles me. A cousin and I loved to wait outside and challenge any youthful visitor to a fight.

I well remember the last fight I had at that old church. My cousin and I often waited outside for young men to enter the doors.

Then, I would challenge one of them to a boxing match. On that particular day, we didn't have to wait long.

My cousin alerted me. "Look, Boogie, here comes someone."

Glancing up I saw three youngsters headed our way.

"Where you boys heading?" I asked.

"We're going down to the spring to get us a drink of water," the older boy responded.

"My grandma doesn't like folks gathering near her spring; she's afraid they will foul the water."

"It's okay," the younger of the three said. "We'll be careful."

Looking them over before challenging either of them to a fight, I decided the middle kid looked to be about my age and size.

Gazing at him with eyes set as threatening as possible, I blurted out. "You want to fight?"

"No," he responded. "Why would I want to fight you?"

The boys turned and continued toward the spring. Now I was sure I had the upper hand. I had challenged him to a fight, and he had refused. Surely, he was afraid of me. He probably knew I could whup him. It wasn't long until we saw them slowly walking back up the hill in our direction. I gathered my courage and wondered what to say to goad him into a fight. They all three walked past us and continued toward the church.

I called out again. "You sure you don't want to fight?"

"No!' he said and continued toward the sound of singing.

"You're nothing but a coward," I shouted.

That pretty much did the trick. He turned, walked away from his companions, and stood firmly facing me. He didn't say a word.

I should point out here that we were around eight to ten years old at the time. A fight back then consisted of challenging your opponent. Once a challenge was accepted, you turned your arm to your opponent and dared them to hit you. Usually, they would cautiously tap you on the shoulder, and in return, you would tap them back. With each tap, you would strike slightly harder until someone submitted, or you would soon be harmlessly rolling around in the dust, grunting and groaning until one or the other, or both, gave up. It usually started with turning your arm to him as if to say, "Here, knock this chip off my shoulder."

I turned, braced myself, and boldly said, "You hit me first."

It immediately became apparent that he didn't know or understand our mountain rules. That first lick wasn't aimed at my shoulder, nor was it a tap as I had expected. It was a devastating wallop delivered upside my head. I thought I might have seen Jesus, at least for a few seconds. I know I saw the stars of heaven exploding and fading repeatedly inside an enormous, empty cavern. Coming to my senses, I cleared the rails as I jumped inside my grandmother's pasture fence, hoping for protection.

Now standing safely a few feet away from my adversary, I called back with the high rail fence between us. "Well, you didn't whip me."

I wasn't sure which of the three I was speaking to. They were all spinning around in my head, which was fuzzy from the blow that "didn't whip me."

The fact was that I had been whipped, and I well knew it, and with only one blow! But pride or stupidity didn't allow me to admit it, so I stood there feeling safe, a dozen feet or so inside my grandmother's pasture.

The older of the three laughed sarcastically and said, "Yeah, you've been whipped and whipped good."

"You're nothing but a liar." I foolishly blurted out.

He climbed across that Virginia-style rail fence with such force that he took off the top two rails and marched to where I stood, panicking! I wanted to run, but my feet wouldn't move. He made one of the biggest fists I have ever seen in my life and shoved it hard against my aching face and nose. I'm sure my eyes crossed as I beheld that giant fist.

"Just dare to say another word," he cautioned.

I didn't! I just stood there, paralyzed with the realization that a simple utterance could terminate my life then and there. He and his two friends returned to their seats in that old church. My cousin and I followed sheepishly behind them, sat on the back pew, and sat quietly. I thought it would be safer inside rather than waiting outside where some brutal kid could possibly maim me for life.

Oddly, I didn't fall under the conviction that day either, but surely seeds were being planted because I did go to church more often and felt lucky to have all my teeth still when doing so. That was the last fight I ever challenged anyone to. After that episode, I found that I was far more comfortable inside the church than out, and that may have been the beginning of my call to salvation.

My grandmother didn't cease to love me, nor did I stop loving her. She continued to pray for my soul after that day in her favorite church. I had hurt her feelings, and I felt terrible, but I didn't feel any salvation coming over me that day, and unfortunately, I didn't see my grandmother much after that. The sawmill at Easy Gap had cut and sawed most of the available timber in that range, so we moved north, toward the end of the mountain, which overlooked the Tennessee River near Camac's Ferry.

Chapter Sixteen
Freight Train Coming

Pinkney and I moved with the sawmill crew into Tennessee and found room and board in one of three railroad line shacks on a mountainside overlooking the tracks of the Great Southern Railroad. Here, a long, high trestle crossed over a deep ravine. From the front porch, we could sit above the tracks and watch the passing trains move slowly up the steep mountain grade and across the trestle at least forty to fifty feet above a small, rushing creek and a narrow roadway parallel to the creek. I watched each time as the engines pulled their heavy loads across that high expanse, imagining that at any moment, it could jump track and crash violently into the valley below.

PHOTO COMPLIMENTS OF GIDEON MOORE

One Saturday after a hard week at the sawmill, Pinkney and I were casually resting and rocking gently in chairs set on the front porch for its boarders. It was an enjoyable day for relaxing and listening to the sounds of nature echoing across the valley below us. Suddenly a ruckus caught our attention and charging up the narrow roadway that came only as far as our line shacks was a wagon pulled by two straining horses, their noses flared and their eyes wild from fright. In the wagon rode three men. The men seemed desperate, and, finding themselves at the end of the road, they jumped from the wagon and searched for a place to hide. At first, they ran toward our house, but seeing us on the porch, they turned and climbed down to the railroad tracks. They then ran toward the high span that crossed the deep gully.

Pinkney and I stood, watching and wondering what had caused the men to act with such desperation. They hurried toward our side of the bridge. Then another group of men, armed with guns, came galloping up and were shouting for the men to halt. The glint of sunlight reflecting off tin badges revealed some were sheriff's deputies. The men from the first wagon didn't stop and kept running toward the high bridge. A shot rang out, and one man staggered and grabbed his leg but continued limping as best as he could toward the crossing. Then, from down the valley, I heard an approaching train's familiar, shrill whistle. All three men had now reached the long expanse of the trestle and were hurrying to cross over. Turning and looking back down the mountain toward the sounds of an approaching train, Pinkney and I could see the thick, rapid puffs of black smoke billowing upwards from the engine's smokestack rising above the screen of trees. Within seconds, the train came into view as it rolled toward the trestle, its whistle blowing repeated warnings. Too late to slow, the engine continued its steady chug-chug of steam as it grew closer. In their desperate attempt to flee, the men had not heard the locomotive now bearing down on them.

It was painful to watch. I reasoned that even criminals deserve a degree of compassion as members of the human race. Now, dozens of feet out on the bridge and with no way to escape, all three realized the time of the Grim Reaper's arrival. The two who could run fled across the track in a frenzied panic, running awkwardly while trying not to step into the openings between the bridge's crossties. The injured man, hobbling along pitifully and well behind his companions, was now exhausted and out of breath. He stopped, gave up, and turned to face death with a final expression of anguish I'll never forget. He stood with outstretched arms as if bracing for the impact against the mighty engine. I shuddered to watch. I heard myself muttering a frantic prayer as the train rolled toward him. Indeed, I thought, as the man faced eternity, he had asked for forgiveness. The engineer finally saw the doomed man on the trestle and applied the brakes, but it was too late. There was too much noise to hear the desperate man's last moment. I watched as his body was swept from the tracks by the cowcatcher. It threw him upward, tumbling in a chaotic somersault. His body fell in a long arch that seemed to plunge in slow motion as it disappeared into the ravine below. Pinkney and I were sickened and emptied our stomachs at the gruesome spectacle.

Steadying myself on one of the porch posts, I straightened to see the two remaining men running hopelessly toward the far side of the trestle. It was clear they weren't going to make it, and it was obvious that they would be pitched from the tracks just as their companion had been. Everyone braced for impact as the train sped toward them, but the men suddenly turned and jumped from the tracks. They had chosen to leap into the deep ravine rather than be crushed under the oncoming Great Southern.

The disbelieving sheriff's deputies all scrambled from the tracks and down the mountainside to find and recover their remains. Pinkney and I quickly followed. We soon found the mangled body of the first victim, who had been knocked from the trestle. He would not have been recognizable even had we known him. Amazingly, his two companions were found injured, but neither had been killed. One had broken both of his legs and a couple of ribs but had been saved after plummeting through a thick canopy of trees and brush that cushioned his fall. The other had the good fortune to have jumped into a deep pool of water in the stream below. He also had a broken leg and was half drowned. He was found floundering after his impact in the deep water. He was revived after a few moments of lying on his stomach with his arm lifted behind his back.

Pinkney and I learned later that the three thugs had stolen the horses and a wagon back near Camac's Ferry and, in their escape, had run over and killed a small child, one that was a favorite in the community. Avoiding death by train and leaping into the chasm didn't help them much in the long run. The two survivors were eventually tried, found guilty of murder, and hanged, broken legs, ribs, and all.

Pinkney and I became familiar with the daily schedule of the trains and found that after one crossed over the bridge, it would be at least a couple of hours before the next one came along. This gave any person who was willing and brave enough to walk over the dizzying heights plenty of time to cross without fear of being knocked from the trestle by an oncoming train. The railroad followed the course of the creek upward and through a low gap and into the valley beyond. A mile beyond the trestle, two important roads came together, and at this intersection, a small, close-knit community had been established before the Civil War. The little village consisted of about three dozen homes, a couple of churches, a mercantile, a post office, and a railroad depot.

The small hamlet was named Angel's Switch after an early settler by the name of Archibald Angel had established his home there soon after the government had removed the last of the Indians from the valley. Angel's Switch's mercantile store included a side room that served as the village post office. There was a railroad depot where the mail was delivered by train before it was transferred to the post office. There was also a doctor's office with an adjoining law office bridgeand even a repair shop for wagons and automobiles. Nowadays, it seemed many families owned either a truck or a car, at least the more affluent ones did, and Angel's Switch was no exception.

Pinkney and I routinely braved the trestle, walking across as swiftly as possible and following the tracks up to the mercantile at Angel's Switch. We purchased necessities such as soap, hair tonic, loaf bread, and a bologna stick for our daily lunches there. We usually checked to see if we had any mail, but rarely did anyone write to us while we were living near the switch. Most everyone who knew us knew we were usually busy at the sawmill. Neither of us had a girlfriend and really hadn't given it much thought until we began to notice that Angel's Switch had an unusual number of pretty girls, with many near our ages. Most were cousins, and unfortunately for the girls, most of the young men living in the community were also brothers or cousins. Pinkney and I didn't mind, thinking it was to our advantage. And neither did the boys from Camac's Ferry or even from Big Grove Mountains, who descended on the village like ants at a sorghum mill to flirt with and try to impress the young ladies. Pinkney and I were no exceptions.

Entering the mercantile one lazy summer afternoon, we found several young men crowding around the postal counter. Anxious to see what the attraction was, I moved through the crowd to get a better view. Standing behind the counter was undoubtedly the prettiest young lady I had ever laid eyes on. Most of the boys, who were older than me, were openly teasing her about whose girl she was going to be. It was obvious she was not amused but embarrassed by their foolish antics. Looking around, I noticed that some of the young men were quite handsome and better dressed than me, and obviously, flirting came naturally to them.

Being shy and not really knowing what to say, I simply asked," Is there any mail for Daniel Blackspaniel?"

She turned to the general delivery box, shuffled through the assorted letters, and returned to the counter.

"Sorry, she said, "There is no mail for any Blackspaniel."

"It's okay," I replied while turning to walk away. "I never get any mail anyway."

"Check again tomorrow," she said. "You could possibly have something by tomorrow."

I stepped away from the counter, and the other guys again crowded toward her and continued to harass her with their nonsense. I stood there, mesmerized, admiring her natural beauty. Then I saw her look up through the crowd, directly at me, and smile sweetly. I felt my heart quicken and my confidence encouraged. With any luck, I would be able to request my mail again on my next visit. I thought of moving through the crowd of admirers again to speak to her but knew that I would only add to the silliness of the other youths. Instead, I walked to a second counter where an older gentleman waited.

"How can I help you?" he asked.

I handed him my brief list and said, "Just a few items, thank you."

"Do you mind if I ask who the young lady who's working behind the postal counter is?"

"Oh, that's Willow. She is my niece. She's been away attending the academy and will be working with me here at the store this summer while on school vacation. Seems to be quite an attraction with all the boys, I see."

I looked back in Willow's direction. She was again lost in the crowd of admirers. I was envious, seeing that several of the young men had no problem boasting of their own potential. I doubted that my patched overalls and country drawl would make much of an impression. But then, I remembered that she had at least cast that promising smile in my direction.

As Pinkney and I walked back along the railroad tracks toward home I must have floated along, completely unaware of my surroundings. I was lost in images of that beautiful young lady at the mercantile store. I must have been dreaming while walking. As we walked home, I didn't even remember crossing the dangerously high trestle over that darkened chasm.

I was well aware of my lack of courting skills. As a matter of fact, I had none. I had never given much thought to girls, except for the two Tisham sisters. They were pretty enough but were forbidden because of their brothers. Meeting Willow for the first time had awakened an excitement inside me that I had never known before.

Willow dominated my thoughts during the following week. Notching a tree with an axe and sawing it with a heavy crosscut can be dangerous if you don't pay attention. More than once, Pinkney scolded me for riding the saw when I became distracted and did not pull the saw smoothly through the cut. Somehow, I made it through the week without maiming myself or Pinkney, which was good. Friday evening found us both butt-deep in wash tubs, readying ourselves for our visit to Angel's Switch.

We usually visited on Saturdays, but I couldn't wait, and we prepared to visit this Friday evening instead. Once we had scrubbed the filth of sweat and sawdust from our bodies, we dressed in our best overalls and hit the tracks toward the switch with our hair well-oiled down. Pinkney had his heart set on one of the young ladies he knew would also be waiting there. As I walked along, I thought over and over what I would say to Willow when I saw her again. I was awkward in conservation and terribly shy, and I found any discussions with the ladies difficult. How could I gain an advantage over all the other young men I expected to find crowding around her?

Entering the mercantile, I noticed that the expected crowd of suitors wasn't there. It seemed that Willow's uncle had finally grown tired of all the boys loitering near the postal counter and being a general nuisance. Only two older youths were lounging near the potbellied stove, talking quietly and leisurely sipping their sodas. Both well-groomed young men watched me as I approached the second counter.

"How can I help you today, young man?" asked Willow's uncle.

I've come for my regular items: soap, bread, and such." I said, looking around for Willow.

"Thought I'd check for any mail while I'm here."

"Willow can help you with that. She'll be back shortly. She ran upstairs to freshen up, I think. The taller fellow over there is her brother, and the other young man is Frankie. Frankie works down at the railroad depot. I think they are waiting for her. Go over and have a seat."

Glancing in their direction, I noticed they conversed casually near the stove's warmth. Sitting silently in the shadows nearby was a young lady.

I felt awkward but seated myself in an extra chair near the girl.

She smiled, leaned toward me, and whispered, "You're new here, aren't you? My name is Ruthie."

"Nice to meet you, Ruthie. I am Daniel Blackspaniel. I'm here to see if I have any mail."

The two young men completely ignored me as I sat down, and they continued with their conversation. I nodded in their direction and then sat silently, waiting for Willow to return.

Her brother, I thought. Maybe I should introduce myself and get acquainted, but just as I started speaking, Willow came down the stairs and the depot guy stood and embraced her. My heart sank! Willow, noticing me, appeared slightly embarrassed and immediately moved behind the postal counter.

"Can I help you, sir?" she asked, looking at me. She appeared uncomfortable as she glanced up in my direction.

Already feeling defeated, I managed to reply, "Yes, remember me, Daniel Blackspaniel? I wanted to check to see if I have any mail today."

Willow turned to the general delivery box and sorted through the loose mail.

"Sorry, again, there is no mail for anyone named Blackspaniel."

I hadn't expected any mail anyway. I was using the mail as an excuse to visit with Willow. Now, I find she obviously has a boyfriend, and my hopes are dashed. But already I'm lost in thoughts of how to overcome her interest in this guy, Frankie, and steal her away.

The following week at work was an emotional one. I couldn't think of anything other than beautiful Willow. I couldn't get her off my mind. I found Pinkney and me hurrying up the railroad tracks toward Angel's Switch on Saturday morning. I felt defeated, but hope still pulled me toward the mercantile. Arriving there, I found several youths milling around outside the store. Most were sipping sodas and laughing at each other's corny jokes.

Approaching the postal counter, I asked, without hope, if there was any mail for anyone named Blackspaniel. Willow, as always, moved to the general delivery box and shuffled through the contents. I was shocked when she returned with a letter for Daniel Blackspaniel. It was with disbelief that I accepted the letter. Oddly, it had no postmark or any return address. Surely, it had been written by my mother or possibly my grandmother but with no return address, I was puzzled. The letter emitted the most pleasant, perfumed scent of lavender. I opened it at once, eager to see who had written me this totally unexpected letter.

It started, "Dear Daniel, you don't know me, but we have met. I think you are too shy to speak, so I thought it best to write to you to break the ice, as they say. Why is it you continue to come to our store and fail to talk to me? I won't bite, you know, at least not hard. You are cute and would like to become better acquainted." It was signed, "Willow Mae Countess."

My heart nearly exploded. I immediately looked up at Willow. She wore a most mischievous but promising smile. Had Willow invited me into her life? Stunned and unsure that I had read the letter correctly the first time, I quickly read it again. Yes, it said what it said. With a lump in my throat, I slowly lowered the page and looked toward Willow. Her deep blue eyes sparkled, and she still wore that mischievous but reassuring smile. I realized that I had been smitten. But wait, I thought. It seemed she already had a suitor and one that felt comfortable enough to embrace her in public. I slowly lowered the letter further and looked questionably in her direction.

"What?" she asked.

"I don't understand. Isn't the depot guy your boyfriend?"

"Oh, you mean Francois Forestier. He is my mother's favorite, not mine. He is a bit pretentious, I'm afraid. He thinks he owns me because our mothers think we're such a great match, and they encourage him at every chance. It is as though I have been pledged without any consideration for myself. Our mothers are in cahoots, determined that we will be married one day. Francois already acts as if he owns me, but in private, he shows me little genuine affection. Francois is French, you know. Mrs. Forestier thinks it is more sophisticated and insists everyone calls him that, but his name is actually Francis. His father is the pastor at our church, and his mother insists that I sit with her during services to keep me separate from any other boys. I feel like a prisoner there."

"Francis works down at the depot handling freight," she continued, "And as a ticket agent for the Great Southern. Most of the girls here at the Switch just swoon over him. My parents, especially my mother, assume that we will marry someday, but I would rather choose for myself who I would spend my life with, and it probably will not be Francois. My parents don't allow anyone other than Francois to call on me. They like the fact that he has a college degree and a steady job down at the depot."

I thought Francois seemed nice enough, possibly a little stuffy, but still nice. I needed an advantage.

"Do you attend church?" she asked.

Caught slightly off guard, I laughed, embarrassed as I thought back to the church incident with my precious Grandmother Blackspaniel.

"Did I say something funny?"

"No, Ma'am, you didn't. Just something that happened recently when I attended church with my grandma."

"So… you do go to church?" she asked with a puzzled smile.

"Yes, I mean no…I mean not all the time. It depends on where our sawmill set is located and how close we are to a church."

"You could join me on Sundays if you like. None of the local boys dared to ask me, knowing that Mother would disapprove and my brother would probably pulverize them. I think if I don't get to see anyone new, I will simply burst. Just when I was most desperate, you came into our store, and now, I see you as my new knight in shining armor, and I have a plan. It calls for daring and a bit of deceit if you are willing to indulge me. You have met my best friend, Ruthie. She and I have a plan. You, Ruthie, and I will attend church together as friends, and you and Ruthie can pretend to have an interest in each other. The plan will work as Mother indulges my rebellious nature enough to allow friends to join us in our pew, knowing I won't misbehave there. Francois works every Sunday at the depot so he can't be there. Of course, you will have to endure the discomfort of sitting between me,

CHURCH AT ANGEL'S SWITCH

Ruthie, my parents, and the pastor's wife. Consider it a penance for some act committed against God's will."

My head was spinning. I was willing to do just about anything to spend time with Willow. I thought it an act of defiance, an adventure, choosing to attend church with the prettiest girl in Angel's Switch even though I would be sitting between two domineering mother hens. I was already enjoying the idea of playing with Willow's subterfuge scheme. It could be fun.

I was momentarily elated with the prospect of joining Willow at church. Then I remembered to my discomfort the fact that I had no nice Sunday go-to-meeting clothes.

Sensing my embarrassment, she asked, "Do you have a problem with sitting near me in church?"

"No, ma'am, I surely don't; it's just that I only have a couple of pairs of overalls, and this ragged pair I'm wearing is probably the best of either."

Willow smiled reassuringly and said, "Well, wash them up clean and run a hot iron over them and we will see you on Sunday morning."

She accompanied me to the door and pointed up toward a pleasant, white-framed house situated a couple hundred yards up the mountainside.

"That's our home up there, the third one with the white picket fence. We will be expecting you by 9:30 A. M. next Sunday morning. Sunday school begins at 10:00, with services at 11:00."

"Meet me there at the gate next Sunday morning then."

"But what about your mom and dad?" I asked.

"Oh, don't worry about them. They will be civil enough since you, Ruthie, and I will be going together as friends. But please be warned, they will assuredly watch and listen to our every move. Remember you're going with two friends to church, not the Saturday night barn dance down at O'Leary's. And remember that my mother is overprotective and will not invite you into our home when you come to our gate, nor will they do so after you walk us home. Only precious Francois is welcome inside our home by them. You can expect them to follow a few paces behind us as chaperones as we walk to church. They will believe that you are more interested in my friend Ruthie, and our charade should prove successful. Now that you know what to expect, are you still willing to escort us to the services?"

I don't think anything could have prevented me from taking part in this seemingly harmless farce.

On Sunday, I arrived several minutes early and nervously paced back and forth in front of the gate. Then, promptly at 9:30, Willow, Ruthie, and her parents walked from their house and joined me there. I noticed the slightly confused expressions on her parents' faces. I am sure they were hopeful that I was truly the suitor of Ruthie and only a friend of their daughter.

As Willow walked toward me, I could feel butterflies fluttering in my stomach. I had truly never seen anything more beautiful. She wore a dress of white cotton from which the sun radiated an angelic glow and I thought of her as an angel. Her auburn curls fell to below her waist, which accented her large deep blue eyes. Her smile melted my heart, and I immediately fell hopelessly in love with her. Her breasts were lost under her homespun garment, but her figure invited admiration. I thought her to be the most stunning vision of a young lady I had ever seen. How could any angel be more beautiful? Me? I had on the best of my two pairs of overalls. They may have been patched here and there but were clean and pressed as suggested. My long-sleeved white shirt was well-ironed and carefully tucked under my overalls. I am sure I impressed her parents as nothing more than a simple country bumpkin. Playing the role of a dear friend of Ruthie was surely going to be the best charade of my life.

The church bells down the valley pealed pleasantly, summoning us to the service. Walking to church on Sunday mornings had become a tradition for Willow's family and many of the other families in Angel's Switch. I was pleased to play my role and enjoyed my conversations with Ruthie while hiding any pretense of speaking with Willow.

As Willow had forecast, her parents walked a few paces behind us and carefully listened to our conversations. To their credit, they allowed us to continue uninterrupted, and they followed us inside the church, where we were met by the pastor and his wife, who greeted us but were confused as to who I was and why I was in the company of their future daughter-in-law and her friend.

Angel's Switch Fellowship Church was a small but beautiful Gothic structure of pure white set against the background of an emerald-green mountain. Its tall steeple reached toward heaven and held a large, brass bell, which I was told had been a gift from the original Angel family. The side windows were tall arches of colored, stained glass. The minister there was not as harsh as at my grandmother's church. His suit fit his slight frame well, reminding me of a penguin and his sermon was far less chafing than the preacher at my grandmother's church. His messages strictly condemned us sinners and were designed to strengthen Christian values and I was far less concerned that he might drop dead from a heart attack.

My attendance there was misguided. I remember little of what the preacher said. My thoughts were for Willow and not for God and I wondered later how God might deal with me. I cannot express my emotions knowing that I was attending church with Willow while pretending that my interest was in Ruthie. Still, the intrigue somehow pleased me.

I heard Mrs. Countess whisper to the pastor's wife, "He is a friend of Ruthie's."

Our deceit was working, and instead of guilt, I had a feeling of accomplishment. With a puzzled expression, the pastor's wife directed us into our seats and promptly seated herself next to Willow in the pew.

Leaning toward Willow, I heard her whisper, "Who is this next to you?"

"Oh, this is Daniel. He is a friend of Ruthie."

Obviously concerned, she straightened and sat looking toward the pastor who approached the pulpit and struggled to begin his sermon. My presence in the company of their presumed future daughter-in-law made them uncomfortable. Willow's parents sat like statues in a trance, embarrassed that I had had the audacity actually to enter the church and sit next to their daughter. Willow seemed to enjoy the mischief, and I found myself feeling only slightly uncomfortable. I dared to visit in the midst of the supporters of my nemesis, Francois, and where I knew that I was unwelcome by everyone except for Willow and Ruthie.

The service was shorter than I had expected. I think the pastor was infuriated that I had boldly sat next to their future daughter-in-law in church. Mrs. Countess shifted uncomfortably in her seat. I noticed that she frequently looked at Willow with the most disapproving facial expressions possible. Willow heroically ignored her. I tried to remain brave, remembering that Willow had not yet committed herself to marriage and she had invited me to go with her on this occasion.

After the service, as we exited, Pastor Forestier neither recognized me nor made eye contact. Nor did he invite me back for future services. Mrs. Forestier leaned toward me and angrily berated me for being so presumptuous as to attend church in the company of their son's fiancé. She had been promised to their son, Francois, and I had embarrassed their family in front of their church members. Willow's parents again walked a few feet behind us but never once spoke to me. Back at the gate, they waited until Willow had said her goodbyes and she and her friend Ruthie returned to their homes, I will admit that I was impressed with Willow's defiance and slightly amused at my own participation. I was determined to go to church with her again if given the chance.

For the first few weeks of our acquaintance, Willow and I talked casually during the times I visited her at the mercantile, and even there her uncle kept a close eye on us. I wasn't allowed to walk her home from the store. Her escort home was usually her friend Ruthie or Francois, and I suspected he was suspicious of my friendship with Ruthie since it was obvious that I mostly talked with Willow. I had never even embraced or kissed her and I felt I was about to burst. I needed time to properly court her and prove my devotion to her. It wasn't long until I had a terrific crush on her, but then so did all the other young men who gathered inside that little mercantile to gush and act foolish.

On weekdays, as Pinkney and I sawed oak, hickory, and pine, Pinkney again had to scold me occasionally for riding the crosscut saw. Cutting big timber requires hard work and concentration and I often found myself lost in thoughts of Willow, daydreaming of winning her from Francois and carrying her away to some castle on a hill. I was a newcomer to Angel's Switch and obviously impressed Mr. and Mrs. Countess as a country dolt whose promise for any girl's future would be a hard life. Her parents had their sights set on Francois, a more sophisticated young man who worked as the ticket agent down at the train depot. He was always well-dressed in slacks, a dress shirt, a tie, and a silly little railroad hat that appeared odd on someone so formally dressed.

Selfishly, I found it amusing when Sunday arrived, and Francois' duties required him to remain at the train station handling freight, selling a few tickets, and receiving any mail arriving for Monday deliveries. I think it was their fear that Willow would totally rebel if not allowed some discretion which allowed me to go with her and Ruthie to church. It should have been of little concern since we were so well chaperoned, but I sensed that both Willow's and Francois' parents were infuriated. I was a replacement since Francois was unable to attend church with their daughter and they begrudgingly accepted me for that reason only. I could live with that, at least for the time being, and I couldn't wait for each Sunday to arrive.

I would show up at their gate in my best-pressed overalls with my brogans wiped clean and my hair oiled down tightly against my head. Their church was only a quarter mile or so distant and unless rain threatened, they always walked. During inclement weather, I knew not to show up at their gate. They always took their surrey, and I was never invited to ride with them. The closeness might allow me to become too familiar with their daughter.

I didn't understand at the time, but my reason for attending church was terribly misguided. Instead of hearing the old minister's message of God, my mind was dominated by thoughts of Willow and the fact that I had the honor of sitting next to the prettiest girl in town. Had lightning struck at that moment I would have been the only soul there not receiving my wings for the flight to heaven.

After the services, while walking with the family back to their home, I would try to think of ways to see Willow alone. As she had earlier cautioned, her parents would never invite me into their home. Nor did I get any invitations to any of the many social events that were sponsored by that little church. My meager attempts to actually talk privately with her were confined to my visits to the mercantile and those were constantly interrupted by an endless parade of suitors and customers. I was growing desperate.

I think the soles of my brogans polished that ole railroad track between our line shack and Angel's Switch just about as much as the four daily trains did, two traveling east and two heading west each day. On the weekdays we found no time for courting and were generally too tired to visit the switch. Me and Pinkney spent a few minutes each evening rocking on the porch of our boarding house and wistfully watching the tracks and listening to the sounds of nature echoing across the valley below us. I often watched the tracks toward Angel's Switch and imagined that Willow would magically appear, her dress billowing in the summer breeze as she walked toward me across the long windy span of that high trestle.

The days and weeks passed far too quickly, and finally, it was announced that we had once again cut all the timber the Cumberland Crosstie Company had contracted for. It was again time to move our sawmill. Knowing that this day was coming, I had dreaded it with every bone in my body. This move would be one of the most painful events of my life. I was saddened that my time with Willow would be decidedly interrupted. We were informed that our new contract was for a large tract of timber approximately forty miles south of Big Grove and well beyond Easy Gap. How, I wondered, could I possibly continue courting the girl of my dreams?

My every thought was of Willow, and my desire was for us to spend the rest of our lives together. Given the chance and under different circumstances, I would have asked her to marry me. Unfortunately, I had failed to gain her parent's approval. They still had their hearts set on Francois and now I was being removed from the equation.

Brokenhearted, I stumbled along the tracks toward Angel's Switch. How was I to tell Willow? Of course, I would promise to return soon and, if possible, renew my efforts to convince her parents that I was the best choice for a son-in-law. Surely love had some importance. I practiced over in my head dozens of ways to break the news, and none seemed adequate. Entering the store, I found Willow behind the counter sorting mail and turning to me she smiled sweetly. My heart melted. I removed a soda from the icebox and collapsed into a chair near the potbellied stove.

"What's wrong Daniel?" she asked.

"Sweetheart, I have sad news. Our mill boss informed us today that we have cut all the timber in our contract here and we will be shutting the mill down and moving to a tract nearly forty miles south of here on Big Grove."

Stunned, Willow's eyes at once flooded with tears, and she slumped to a bench behind the counter. "Oh Daniel, no! Please don't tell me you are leaving," she cried.

"Sweetheart, I have no choice. We will be working at Grandpa Blackspaniel's mill where our family has a new contract. I don't see any way out of moving."

"Durn you, Daniel. Please don't do this to me. Don't abandon me now. Just when I thought I might not have to marry that boring Francois. Now you are leaving! What am I supposed to do?'

"Willow, I'll be back soon, just as soon as we get the sawmill set, I'll come back. I promise I'll write you every week." And I'll be back shortly, even if I have to walk the whole way, I'll be back."

I stood and walked to her but she clenched her fist and repeatedly struck my chest.

"Durn you, Daniel, please don't do this to me," she repeated.

Tears of despair washed down her cheeks as she threw her arms around me and embraced me in desperation. Then, turning, she rushed upstairs while crying her heart out.

Chapter Seventeen
Billows of Smoke and Soot

It took the better part of two weeks to move and set up our sawmill. We were in one of the most isolated rural areas that I ever worked. Our company had received a contract to cut a large tract of timber belonging to a family named Overdeer. Thankfully, the Blackspaniel family, including my friend Pinkney, were fortunate enough to arrange room and board with the Senior Overdeer's son, Jesse, who lived with his wife, two young sons, and his grandmother on the original family farm miles from the closest neighbor. The home in which we boarded was the original Overdeer homestead. It was a large, two-story frame house that had been the residence of four generations of the Overdeer family for most of eighty years. Naturally, death and marriage had reduced the number of occupants to those five remaining family members. There was plenty of room for us boarders. Pinkney, June Bug, and I shared a room on the upper floor, and my sisters shared a room with Granny Overdeer down the hall from us. From the second-story porch, we could relax and watch the cows graze over the brown pastures of early autumn. I enjoyed the temporary distractions while looking out over the fertile fields and listening to the sounds of the wind rustling through several tall, hundred-year-old oaks that stood as sentinels in the yard.

As promised, I wrote my first letter to my dear Willow and deposited it in the family mailbox at the end of the long farm lane. I wondered how long before I would hear back from her in return. The next few days found us busy in the woods and I had little time to think about letters except for being anxious to hear back from Willow. I fully expected that within a week I would receive a response to my letter to her. Returning from work each day, I hurried to Mrs. Overdeer to ask if I had received any mail.

"Sorry, Daniel, you have not," she would reply.

I hurried to write another letter and place it in the postal box then waited another week. Unfortunately, I heard nothing from Willow. I began making plans to travel forty miles to see her at the first opportunity.

It was late fall and the weather had been most agreeable, warmer than expected, and after another exhausting day in the woods, Pinkney and I rested on that upper porch. I wondered again why I hadn't heard from my girl. Quail called back and forth from hidden places in the tall grass until a pair of owls hooted to each other as evening began to darken the sky. All I could think of was Willow. A dog barked off in the distance and I wondered where its family lived. The Overdeers had no near neighbors and their hounds were resting on the lower porch. I was distraught. Without the company of Willow, my world was falling apart.

"Hey, Daniel; hey Pinkney," Grandma Overdeer said as she walked to the porch.

"Hi, Grandma," I barely grunted.

"It's pleasant here, isn't it?" she suggested.

"Yes, ma'am, it is. This is a beautiful farm, one that I could live on for the rest of my life," I said, thinking of Willow.

We all rocked gently, each lost in our thoughts while looking out into the growing darkness.

"My goodness," she said," It's turning cool. I hadn't noticed the chill until now."

"Neither had I, grandma," I answered. "I see the clouds are beginning to hide the stars. Tomorrow may be a cold one."

She got up and excused herself, "Going in now boys. I'll see you in the morning. You better throw an extra quilt over your bed tonight."

A breeze swept through the trees and across the porch bringing with it the hints of an early winter. I got up from my chair, went into my bedroom, and turned down my quilt.

"We may need heavier clothing tomorrow," I told Pinkney.

Morning arrived with an unprecedented drop in temperature, far more than expected. It was downright cold; the thermometer had dropped from sixty-eight down to thirty-two in a matter of hours and that was just the beginning.

"I don't remember the wooly worms predicting this," Granny said.

It was the winter of 1937, and the first few weeks were reasonably warm and pleasant. Working in the timber belonging to Mr. Overdeer had dominated our thoughts and kept us preoccupied. Then, looking up through the bare branches, I noticed the sky blanketed with dark, gray clouds. The wind gathered in intensity and soon howled through the branches, causing them to sway back and forth with a chaotic rhythm. It grew colder and colder, and Grandpa warned that we should probably return to the farm and prepare for the major storm that was surely coming.

Already, snow floated earthward from the heavens. Within hours, it had turned bitterly cold. A wall thermometer where our family boarded showed forty-two degrees Fahrenheit, and that was on the interior wall inside the house. Most repairs to the old house had been put off or neglected over the years, and now it was proving inadequate to provide warmth for the people living there. Outside, the temperature continued to drop until it fell to eighteen degrees. The snow had accumulated to a depth of thirteen inches in just a few hours, and it was still coming down. As the wind howled outside with a ferocious intensity, the children and older folks huddled in front of the fireplace in an attempt to conserve and share warmth. Everyone wore their warmest coats, wrapped themselves in quilts, and looked like Eskimos crowded together. Mrs. Overdeer and Mrs. Blackspaniel were busy in the kitchen warming soup to nourish the family when the men returned from gathering wood.

Papa, Uncle Ernest, Mr. Overdeer, and us boys had waded through the snow to the edge of a woodlot to cut and split extra firewood we knew would be needed before this storm was over. We took the time to hitch the horses to our wagon, and as the wind howled, we set to work. Trying to make the best of a bad situation, Mr. Overdeer joked that we would need a stack as tall as his house to warm up in this storm. With our hands near freezing, we busied ourselves with cutting and loading our wagon with all the wood we could gather.

The children, too young to understand the nature of chimney fires, naturally tossed in more kindling as the temperature dropped, and now the fire roared. Unfortunately, the draft prevented the large rooms with lofty ceilings from warming properly, and Grandma and the children sat shivering. Grandma thoughtfully placed a pan of milk near the coals to make hot chocolate for the children and then went to the kitchen to collect cups for the chocolate. In her absence, one of the freezing children carelessly tossed a large chunk of rich pine known as fat lighter into the flames. Now, the fireplace began to burn with an intensity that radiated heat to those closest to the flames and finally, the family felt the warmth. The addition of fat lighter was like adding a cauldron of boiling tar to a brush pile. It quickly became a roaring inferno as flames shot up from the top of the chimney and rained down as chunks of burning creosote. The intensity of the fire forced flames through voids in the chinking and into the attic where old papers and family heirlooms had been stored for years. The burning embers quickly ignited those treasured relics and now the old house began to burn.

As Granny and the children innocently sipped their warm chocolate, they were unaware of the fire burning in the attic above them or of the intense smoke billowing from the roof. Then, Granny noticed the noise of a tremendous whoosh roaring inside the chimney. She had seen chimney fires before. The chimney began to quake, and chunks of creosote now fell back to the fire, adding to the pandemonium. The children, realizing something frightening was happening, jumped to their feet and cried out. Granny called Mrs. Overdeer and Mrs. Blackspaniel from the kitchen and ushered them quickly out the door. Once everyone was outside and presumably safe, she suddenly bolted and ran back inside the burning home. Everyone was calling loudly for her to come out.

Papa, Uncle Ernest, Mr. Overdeer, and Pinkney were busy cutting wood while June Bug, Mr. Overdeer's son, and I carried it to the wagon. Suddenly, papa hesitated. He sensed something was wrong. He turned, looking into the storm. Papa said later that as he was about to toss another armload of wood into the wagon he glanced up and noticed a plume of dirty brown smoke rising above the trees in the direction of the Overdeer house. He stood there for a second, then dropped his load of wood and quickly climbed into the half-loaded wagon.

"Boys, he hollered, jump in! It looks like the Overdeer house is on fire!"

We instantly dropped our axes, saws, and firewood and climbed into the wagon, and Papa started his horses running toward the column of smoke. At the first clearing through the trees, we could see flames shooting from the roof of the old farmhouse. Arriving at the front yard, we found that the women and children were gathered in the yard carrying whatever quilts, blankets, and clothing they could gather.

"Go find grandma," they pleaded. "She is still in there."

We ran through the smoke and found her confused and frightened. She held that big pot of soup the other women had been heating for our lunch in her arms. The men lifted her, soup, ladle, and all, and carried her to the safety of the yard. Realizing she was safe, she began ladling the hot soup to the lips of each of the hungry children. At that point, the upper floor was fully engulfed.

Papa and Mr. Overdeer instructed us boys, "Hurry to the cellar and save what you can. It will be a hard winter if we don't. We'll watch and call you out when it gets too dangerous."

Mr. Overdeer quickly removed all his farm animals safely from the barn, hitched his own wagon to his mules, and pulled it to the hall to be loaded with hay.

Pinkney, June Bug, and I ran to the cellar, threw open the door, and began handing out anything we could lay our hands on. Jars of canned goods, fruit, and vegetables. Flats of apples wrapped in paper—jugs of cider, and even a couple of crocks of homebrew. Papa and Uncle Ernest carefully placed everything on layers of straw spread over the wagon beds. The wagon was still partially filled with firewood, but he would need all the firewood he could get. Papa then called us out of the cellar. The floor above us was burning.

Grandma looked around in disbelief and cried out, "Oh lordy, what will we do?"

Within minutes, the whole house was fully engulfed, and a dark tornado of smoke and soot swirled into the sky to be swept away by the wintry gale. Dirty, black ashes fell into the snow, creating surreal images. Eighty years of aging tinder stacked two stories high now burned with a raging intensity I could have never imagined.

Mr. Overdeer was concerned with his barn and its loft piled high with dry hay. It was just a matter of time until a spark would ignite another inferno. He instructed us to pull our wagons to the barn and fill them with as much hay as possible. We carefully placed the loose hay around the jugs and jars we had removed from the cellar. We would need the hay for warm bedding and horse fodder. Once the hay was loaded, he instructed us to move the wagons to a safe distance upwind of the burning house. Papa had his team of logging mules hitched to the second wagon, and we also loaded it with hay; He then told us to go to the smokehouse and retrieve all the hams and other food items that were stored there.

I will never forget the bewildered expressions those poor children wore while watching their beloved home being consumed by fire. With great sadness, we watched as it burned and finally collapsed into the depths of the cellar. The house, barn, and all the outbuildings were a total loss. As the flames reached into the heavens, the howling winds occasionally fanned them against all the structures. There was nothing we could do but watch and weep. Nothing remained except smoking heaps of ashes and the blackened skeletons of scorched oaks.

We helped Grandma and all the children into the wagon and covered them with layers of hay and blankets. Now, we wondered where in God's name we would go.

Jesse and his family would move in with his parents, but there was no room available for the Blackspaniel family. What would we do? We lost most of our belongings except what we wore and the tools we abandoned in the snow. We saved food from the cellar and smokehouse and our horses, mules, and wagons. Where would we live now? We still had the tract of timber that we had contracted to harvest.

We needed a place close enough to the tract we were cutting. Papa thought for a moment and then remembered his Great-uncle John Rice. His home was miles closer than ours but was still too many miles north for a daily commute. The Rice place was off the mountain and across the Tennessee River at Mud Creek, nearly twelve miles distant. The women and children could stay there and we men could stay in temporary shelters on the Overdeer tract and commute to Uncle John's and visit our family on the weekends, at least until we had a chance to construct a suitable kitchen and bedroom for papa and grandma and a bunkhouse for the workers on the Overdeer tract.

Papa knew that his uncle John had a recently vacated rental house in the valley of Mud Creek. Papa needed to contact Uncle John before he found new renters and arrange for us to stay there until adequate quarters for our work crew near the Overdeer tract could be built.

Papa Blackspaniel asked me if I would ride to Mud Creek and inquire if our family could stay there for a few weeks. I said yes. I was considerably worried for our poor family. Papa drew me a map showing me the route I should take. It was marked with a large X designating a spring where a family named Wooten lived. The spring was a well-known camping site for travelers coming and going between the mountain and the ferry travelers used to cross the Tennessee River. He removed five dollars from his vest pocket to pay for a night's board with the Wooten family and the ferry crossing. The Wootens also owned and operated the ferry. I knew there was no time to waste, so I saddled Papa's mare, bade everyone farewell, and rode southwest toward the gap and off the mountain toward the river and Mud Creek.

Grandma, along with Great-Grandmother and the children, were warmer on the ride to Mud Creek than after the Overdeer fire. Papa layered the bed of the wagons with dried straw and the family sort of burrowed themselves underneath like gophers in their holes. He covered all this with blankets and a protective oilcloth. A smiling great-grandmother later confessed it was the warmest she had been in days.

I rode Papa's mare along steadily, allowing her to choose her own path, and go at her own pace. She knew the way better than me. I am sure Papa has ridden her to Uncle John's many times over the years. It also seemed she sensed the importance of our mission. She occasionally slipped in the snow but never stumbled and we made our way off the mountain without incident. Late in the evening of the first day, I arrived at Wooten's spring and campground. The Wootens lived in a handsome, two-story log structure set on a flat limestone ledge just above a large spring flowing from the base of Big Grove Mountain. From their front porch, they had a panoramic view of nearly a hundred acres of fields where they had recently harvested corn, sugar cane, and tobacco. The Wooten place has been a convenient camping place for travelers for ages, including Indians who camped around the spring. Arrowheads, mortars, and pestles have been found scattered in abundance in the fields proving that it had been a favorite place for them, too.

The Wootens were a good Christian family, always making travelers welcome at their home. Pilgrims often lingered for days there while resting near the soothing sounds of the gurgling water and the cool, refreshing air that flowed from a small cave. No matter to the Wootens, friends and strangers alike were reasons to celebrate, strum a banjo, or play a fiddle and enjoy good old-fashioned Appalachian singing.

When I arrived, several of the family members were busy with their chores and all greeted me with a hearty hello. After introducing myself, I was invited to stay the night and have supper with them. I explained my purpose of traveling in such an unexpected storm and told them Papa and our family should be following me in a day or two. Mr. Wooten was already acquainted with Papa and Uncle Ernest; they had cut timber off the mountainside above his farm years ago and Grandpa helped clear the extensive fields in front. He is a long-time friend of Uncle John. Mr. Wooten said they had served together on a sensational jury trial years earlier.

Later in the evening, Mr. Wooten called his family together and each took a seat around a long dinner table. Taking the nearest one's hand, he asked for God's blessing for our food and me. I was pleased that he also requested blessings for the Blackspaniel family as they journeyed off the mountain. I felt perfectly at ease while visiting with him and his kin. They provided me with a delicious meal and a warm, although slightly crowded bed. As necessity often dictated within large families, I was relegated to sleep between two of his younger sons. Three in a bed together keeps you warm and I slept comfortably once the boys settled down. Excited to have company, they jabbered well into the night. It was only after repeated warnings from their papa to quieten down that they finally stopped their nonsense and we managed to fall asleep. I think they enjoyed my company as much as I enjoyed sleeping in a warm bed amongst friends.

After breakfast, I thanked the family, said farewell, and saddled Papa's mare to continue my journey toward Uncle John's. I was accompanied by one of the older sons, the one that ran the ferry, and together we rode toward the river. He was an interesting young man, easy to laugh and knowledgeable of the history of the area. I enjoyed his many stories. After reaching the river, we maneuvered the ferry into the water and began the long pull across the fast, flowing stream.

My companion informed me that his family also farmed on three of the islands in the middle of the Tennessee River, one of which we were then passing near its southern end. He said the state required all ferries operating on the river to be permitted, and by law, the ferryman should deliver anyone who requested it to the opposite shore. For this service, they were allowed to collect a small fee. Hearing of the fee, I realized I hadn't paid for my board last night nor for the ferry ride. I forgot because I was so caught up in reaching Mud Creek and securing winter quarters for our family.

When I offered, I was told, "Don't worry about it. We understand that your family recently lost almost everything in the fire, and Papa said it is our Christian duty to help in any way we can."

I was thinking about the goodness of many people in the world and the great Christian example the Wooten family presented. I also remembered the ugliness in the hearts of others, such as the Tishams. And then he shared a story of the history of his area.

"See that Island up there?" he asked, pointing upstream toward the island. "We farm that island too, but it gives me the creeps every time we work there. It has a sad and tragic history."

"Why? What happened?" I asked looking toward the island as we pulled at the ropes.

"Forty or fifty years ago it was the scene of several grisly murders."

I straightened and turned toward the island which was still shrouded in an eerie morning mist.

"You're kidding, right?" Now I was shaken. I strained to see through the veil of fog and snow for any ghostly figures that might still be lingering in the canebrakes.

"What happened?" I asked as a chill ran down my spine.

"See that thicket of bamboo?" he said pointing toward the island. "The thicket was much denser back years ago and, at that time, covered much of the island. A family of bootleggers had built their home there and established a large whiskey operation in the brakes which was well hidden in the interior of the cane. They managed to keep their location a secret for most of the three years. They worked the still at night and anytime the fog shrouded the river bottoms to keep any smoke from revealing their location."

"The family consisted of four brothers and their wives, all of whom lived on the island. They cleverly sunk their boats in the shallow water to conceal them from passing fishermen anytime a run was being cooked off. When the shine was ready, they simply salvaged the submerged vessels and used them to ferry their goods to their customers who waited under the guise of fishing, or the crews of passing riverboats. Occasionally an unlucky customer, after becoming inebriated, would stumble from his pirogue and either flounder or drown. The island became known locally as Flounder's Island. The islanders became known up and down the river because of this. It brought them fame and that may have led to their downfall."

"The problem was that the older, established moonshiners back in the mountains highly begrudged the loss of their revenue to the island's bootleggers. Eventually, the mountain moonshiners were able to discover where the island gang had their operation. One moonlit night they rowed quietly across the river and climbed the banks of the island. After a thorough search, they found the hidden cabin and the still. Unfortunately, the mountain men had no intention of simply destroying the still but had agreed to eliminate the competition altogether."

"They caught the unsuspecting islanders completely off guard and, at gunpoint, offered to remove them to the mainland. They told them that they intended to destroy their still and warned them never to return to the island. Under the guise of removing them, they led the unsuspecting residents down the muddy riverbank. When the islanders realized the seriousness of their situation, they begged the mountaineers to allow them to leave the island, promising never to return. The mountain men had no intention of allowing them to leave alive. Standing them waist-deep in the frigid water, they then executed them one by one by shooting them in the backs of their heads. Rocks were then placed inside their body cavities as weights, and each corpse was carried deeper into the current and allowed to sink slowly while the flow of the river carried them several feet away as they sank. Later a couple of the corpses somehow rose to the surface and the grisly murders were discovered. There are still many who believe the profits from all that business are buried on the island. Holes are often left empty by fortune seekers digging there, but I'll not hunt there for fear it is haunted. And there has always since been a rumor that the youngest brother and his wife managed to escape, hiding for days in the thickness of the canebrakes never to be seen again. I'll never forget the name of Tisham!"

Stunned, I just stared toward the island and thought, surely there is no way there is a connection.

He added, "As I remember, Wash Tisham was the younger brother's name."

And then, "It was the trial for those murders that my father and your uncle John Rice served on years ago."

A chill ran down my spine and I watched the shadows more closely, imagining the horror the family had suffered. I guessed that that is what made the Tishams so mean. Whisky and the trouble it brings! For some reason, I couldn't muster the courage to tell him I thought I may know what became of the youngest member of the original Tisham clan.

We reached the far bank, and I mounted my mare and disembarked the ferry. The Wooten youth pointed to a large bell attached to a tall pole and told me to ring that bell loudly when I returned, and he would cross over to pick me up. I rode along in the deep snow with my face wrapped like a mummy. I was still thinking of those grisly murders and wondered if the latest members of the Tisham clan had been caught yet. I also wondered if Willow had received my letters and if she had written back to me. I rode along thinking of all the meanness in the world and if it could be balanced by good. I checked Papa's map often as I rode along, and finally, I arrived at the farm of Uncle John Rice. I thought of my grandparents and the other family members and how they were coming along in the wagons. The road off the mountain would surely be hazardous and I was worried for their safety.

John Rice was a kindly old man. He greeted me with open arms, assured me that our family would be welcome and encouraged me to bring them there as soon as possible. When arrangements were made with Uncle John, I returned to the path toward the ferry. The rope to the bell was encrusted in ice which creaked weirdly as I tugged at it to summon the ferryman. I was returning to help my family as needed. Again, I watched the banks of Flounder's Island with suspicion as we passed back toward the river's eastern bank.

On arriving at the Wooten's residence, we could see two wagons approaching a mile or so in the distance, their dark shapes easily distinguished against the backdrop of fields and brush encrusted with snow. It appeared my family had made it and hopefully was safe. I rode toward them accompanied by two of Mr. Wooten's sons.

Papa and our family received a warm welcome from the Wooten family. They offered any assistance they could give. Papa refused his offer to stay the night. There were too many of us and we needed to get on to Uncle John's as quickly as possible. In the company of the ferry operator, we continued toward the landing. Two teams and two wagons crossing over the river required two crossings and as I waited at the southern landing with Papa, I asked if he remembered the story of the island's grisly history. He said yes, reminding me that he had served on the jury during the murder trial. Most of the older folks still remembered the tale, but he shied away from discussing it further for the fear and anxiety it would cause the children. I asked nothing more.

Our family successfully moved into Uncle John's rental house and after a week, when everyone had become reasonably comfortable, we loaded our wagons and returned to Big Grove. It was difficult going because a torturous layer of snow still covered the earth. It took time to build a kitchen and bunkhouse before our mission of harvesting the timber could begin. Our residence for the first week was a canvas tent set up near the sawmill. It would serve as our home while the more substantial board shacks could be completed. I was reminded of my and Johnny Smothers's visit to Camp Benning down in Georgia. I dubbed our new home, "Camp Slushy."

At every opportunity, I hurried to Mr. Overdeer's mailbox which now stood as the last reminder of a once-magnificent home and farm belonging to one of the last original families in the area. Sadly, there was no mail. Checking later with the Overdeer family, I was informed that no mail had come for me. I had a sickening feeling in my stomach. What could have gone wrong? I was bewildered. Weeks went by and the snow began to melt. Granny returned to the mountain and was now serving up much-appreciated meals for the crew. Going into the woods each morning wasn't as hard now but returning to the mailbox each evening became harder and harder. I was losing hope.

    The women and children waited out the winter at Mud Creek, being entertained by Uncle John. He seemed to enjoy having the children there. The men stayed busy cutting and sawing a forest of virgin timber. Huge trees were felled, sawed, and hauled to a rail station in the little port town of Arcade, Alabama. From there, they were loaded onto river barges and shipped downriver to ports unknown. Our supply of timber seems endless, and now my letters to Willow have slowed. I wrote one last letter to Willow and personally handed it to the mail carrier. He assured me that my letter would be sent through the proper channels.

    I often checked with the Overdeer family to see if any letters had come for me, but sadly, none had. I couldn't understand and remained heartbroken. Forty to fifty miles was quite a distance to travel in the winter, but I found myself preparing for that possibility. And then there was the great thaw. The weather finally warmed, the snow began to melt, ditches and rivers filled, and then flooded over their banks. Getting to Willow now would at least be difficult and probably impossible. Then Grandpa announced that our commitment to Mr. Overdeer was complete. Now we would move the sawmill north again as soon as the water drained, and the roads were drier. Papa said we would move to a cove nestled in the shadows of Grace Mountain. Sadly, I experienced joy and disappointment in turn.

"Lord, please dry up this flood. I prayed that then I could be closer to Willow than at any time in almost a year. It has been too long! I need to find out why she hasn't written to me. First, we will have to get our mill situated, and then I can travel north to Angle's Switch.

When we finally reached the cove it proved to be one of the most breathtaking locations nature could have provided. It was a beautiful estuary surrounded by steep elevations of the mountain that are crowned along their upper heights with towering buff and gray sandstone cliffs. Every ravine sparkled with churning, splashing streams. Everywhere, meadows bloomed with carpets of colorful flowers covering the hillsides. Birds, butterflies, and wildlife abounded, and life's calls and sounds provided the most charming entertainment. Best of all, at least for a timberman, the hills and hollows were thick with old-growth forest, ripe for the taking.

I plan to visit Willow as soon as Papa Blackspaniel can spare me. I will renew my courtship and learn the reason why she has failed to answer my many letters to her. I can also visit my family at Five Corners, which is on top of the mountain above us. Our mill set is just a few yards upstream from a magnificent waterfall about fifteen feet high and thirty wide. Just below the falls are the ruins of a long-abandoned grist or sawmill that we were told predated the Civil War, and during the war, thousands of soldiers had tromped past. The remnants evoked thoughts of the history embedded there and the lost treasures still buried underneath. The stone pillars stand as monuments to the original mill that once flourished on the site. All this and thoughts of Willow caused an excitement in me that cannot easily be extinguished.

I was surprised today when Uncle Ernest arrived and announced that he would be working with Papa and the other lumbermen who were cutting and hauling timber off the mountainside and ridges above our mill. He had previously arranged to rent an old cabin located on an elevation just above the mill, and he invited Pinkney and me to stay there with him and his family. We will still pay for our room and board, and we will be within a short walk of the sawmill. This site seems like a perfect paradise. I am pleased to be working with Uncle Ernest, Papa, Pinkney, and all of our old crew. I am more content now than I have been in months.

The ridges around us are rich in iron ore and the mountains abound in coal. Just a couple of miles further southwest is the Alabama and Georgia Iron Works. Our mill provides the crossties used on the tracks of a small gauge railroad that hauls coal and iron ore from the ridges to the furnace. I think the iron works and the coal and iron mining are all under the ownership of the railroad. We are busier now than ever, but I love it here, I love the history of the area and the people who live in the hills scattered around us.

A town has grown up around the ironworks and is called Benge. A large number of poor white and poorer black families have moved into the community and are employed by the works. One enormous and boastful man claims to be descended from the native Indians that lived here long before any of us white men came. He told us that Chief Benge of the Cherokee people had been a great-great uncle of his, and because of his size, no one dared to dispute his word. Plus, a large open field in the community has long been known as Benge's Field and was supposedly named for his famous uncle.

The town of Benge is bustling with activity. Men are cutting timber and snaking logs off the ridges and the mountainside. Others are digging coal and mining iron ore and railcars are hauling it back to the ironworks. Black smoke billows constantly from the towering twin chimney stacks at the furnace. The town of Benge has a train depot for the Great Southern, a hotel, a large commissary, two churches, a masonic lodge, a distillery, and a half dozen saloons. There are plenty of boarding houses scattered across the valley for all the different tradesmen. It has become a boomtown and is starting to rival Centerville as the busiest small town around. And, of course, one can get into so much mischief here.

It seems to me that our work is as hard as ever, but our minds are soothed by our beautiful, panoramic surroundings. Above the waterfall lies a series of bubbling springs issuing from several small and mysterious crevices. A refreshing breeze blows from the caves and across the springs cooling the air where we labor. We have often seen people come there alone, partially undress, wade into the invigorating waters, and sit as if in a state of euphoria. At other times, small groups appear and bathe quietly. I suppose there must be something miraculous about the springs.

Uncle Ernest announced one evening at the supper table, "Boys, I've discovered some of the most magnificent chestnut and walnut trees

I've ever found on these ridges. I have painted markers on the largest and have instructed my crews not to cut those but to leave them for posterity and re-seeding. It would be a shame if those monuments were lost to our grandchildren."

I loved those old trees myself and felt a sense of pride in my uncle. Chestnuts are my favorite trees, and I wanted to see those giants scattered through the forest forever. That may come to pass as I have been told that a chestnut tree can live for an astounding eight hundred years.

"And another thing," he continued, "I've never seen so many entrances to caves as I have found up in those limestone ledges. I dropped rocks into them and waited for them to hit bottom and I think there may be thirty, fifty, or a hundred or more feet deep. If you are not careful, you could lose a mule up there."

Caves? I have never given much thought to caves. June Bug, Gerty Goforth, and I had crawled into a couple of holes we called caves in the ledges back at Craig's Ridge, but they were dark and intimidating to me. Maybe it would be fun to go back and visit again. Unfortunately, we can hardly keep pace with the wagon loads of logs being delivered to the mill. We were usually too tired to climb through those jagged rocks at the end of the work week. For most of our crew, it is easier to climb into a wagon and ride into Benge to visit one of their busy saloons and sip a beer.

I was puzzled one Friday evening when a couple of the mill workers ushered me to the spring and handed me a bar of soap and a towel.

"Here, Boogie," they said, appearing amused. "Scrub up. We have a surprise for you."

I wondered about the surprise. It wasn't my birthday so what mischief were they up to? I washed my hair, my face, under my arms, and most of the rest of me while they stood nearby with goofy grins on their faces.

"What is up?" I asked. "This better be legitimate," I warned. "I am in no mood for foolishness!"

"Boogie, we've decided it's time for you to go out. You've been too miserable for too long now."

"Come have a beer with us down at Benge's Saloon. We have something to show you."

I must admit I was ready for a night out and a diversion, but I have yet to acquire a taste for alcohol, beer, or whiskey. Still, I thought it would be fun to spend an evening out with my friends.

I dressed in my best overalls, and we loaded into one of our wagons and rode to the town of Benge and into Benge's Saloon. I noticed Pinkney appeared as puzzled as I was.

When we arrived at the saloon, my buddies requested and were given a table near the stage. I was still ignorant as to our purpose there.

One of the more popular attractions of late has been a highly provocative dancer who showed up one weekend and became many of the customers' favorites. She entertains drunken lumbermen and ironworkers with half-naked belly dances. But what did she have to do with me?

After a few minutes of cheering, laughing, and bar-thumping a three-man band began playing a hard-driving, slightly raunchy dance number with overtones from the Orient. Then a scantily-clad young lady emerged shyly from behind a curtain and began to twist and gyrate to the beat of a drum, trumpet, and piano. Her audience cheered and hooped with wild abandonment.

I noticed that my buddies often glanced in my direction as if seeking my approval. Odd, I thought. What did I have to do with her performance? More surprisingly, after the show, she walked to our table and, without an invitation, sat in my lap. My buddies, except for Pinkney, applauded with approval. It seemed that I had been set up. I immediately pushed her from my lap, apologized, and told her I had a girl. I was not yet over my beloved Willow.

As it turned out, she had been encouraged by a few of my buddies, who were concerned with my constant sadness for Willow and wanted to create a distraction. At first, I was angry, but then I understood that, though misguided, they had had the best of intentions. After all was said and done, I was more determined than ever to return to Angel's Switch and Willow.

The Church ladies from Benge strongly objected to the gyrations at the saloon. They Declared her wild form of entertainment on Saturday nights far too offensive and petitioned the sheriff to shut down hers. Sunday church services often bordered on rebellion. The sheriff had one main complication when removing her from the saloon: that hulk of a man who claimed to be the descendant of Ole Chief

Benge. It seems he had a crush on her. I understand that two deputies were injured in the resulting melee.

Chapter Eighteen

A Gentle Giant

While I was planning my trip back to Angel's Switch, an unexpected distraction rolled into town. The mayor and aldermen of Benge had granted permission for a small carnival to set up their tents and exhibits there. Papa told me that our sawmill received the request for sawdust and shavings to cover all the midways and he needed Pinkney and me to deliver and spread several wagon loads. I could go see Willow after that.

Carnivals were always a big attraction when they came to any small town and were attended by folks from miles around. The one that arrived at Benge that year had a special attraction: a large, gentle elephant named Ellen. Of course, she was the largest animal I had ever seen. I thought she was really old because of all her wrinkles and sad because her eyes always seemed to be moist with tears. I wondered if it was because she had no other pachyderm friends. I had always enjoyed animals, and that is one of the reasons that, in my younger days, I had been determined to go to Brazil. But Brazil had no elephants. Probably the closest to one would have been the tapirs and I remembered that they were more akin to rhinos than elephants. On Saturday, the week the carnival was set up, I walked down the wood shavings paths and enjoyed the sideshows. I had the advantage of seeing many of the sights from behind the scenes because all the loads of wood shavings had been purchased from our sawmill, and Pinkney and I helped deliver and spread them.

That is how Ellen and I became acquainted. I was shoveling shavings from our wagon when someone tapped me on the shoulder. Turning, I was startled to see the long extension of her trunk twisting toward me. I jumped back in disbelief.

"Don't be alarmed," her handler said. "She's a gentle giant."

He walked under her massive head, and she pulled him tenderly to herself as if giving him a big, loving hug.

"Her name is Ellen," he said. "She has been with me for almost twenty years now, traveling around the country. It's time for her walk.

He removed her from her enclosure most mornings and allowed her to walk and graze if forage was available.

"Walk with us for a few minutes; she would enjoy your company."

I couldn't resist. Walking with an elephant! I couldn't wait to tell my brother June Bug and our sisters.

Ellen grazed down the gentle slope of the hill and was soon approaching a neighbor's flower garden. We watched from a distance as she deliberately eased toward a patch of color. I honestly think she believed that by moving inch by inch, she thought no one would notice.

Just as she swept a trunk full of pansies toward her mouth, her trainer called out, "Ellen!"

Without hesitation, she quickly stepped away from the flowerbed and continued eating mouths full of grass as innocent as ever, as if to say, "That wasn't me you caught about to eat those pansies."

One of the newer carnival rides was called a Tilt-a-Whirl and the children loved it. I avoided it because all that movement, the twisting and turning, made me queasy, and I usually ended up embarrassing myself by puking my guts out. I did enjoy being on the Ferris wheel; I loved riding to the top and watching all the ant-sized people scurrying around on the ground. I was seated at the very top when I saw my girl, Willow, Ruthie, and Willow's parents watching the children as they rode on the Tilt-a-Whirl. I almost panicked and could have jumped from that great height to get her attention. I yelled and waved my arms frantically, but they never looked up. They were too intent on watching the children on the ride as it bobbed, twisted, rose, and fell. All the screams of joy and laughter drowned out my desperate calls and I watched as they turned and disappeared into the crowd.

Regrettably, the assembly of the Tilt-a-Whirl had been careless and hasty. That night as bright lights flashed, and music mingled with children's laughter filled the air a bolt came loose, and the Tilt-a Whirl crashed to the ground, trapping three small children underneath. The power was cut and from my high perch I could only watch as Willow disappeared into the darkness and as the drama of the broken carnival ride unfolded below me. Parents and promoters alike panicked, and everyone rushed around in disbelief.

Seeing Willow for those few moments added to the ache of my broken heart. I had little chance of ever gaining the consent of her parents. My attention returned to the disaster unfolding below me. Our first priority was to rescue those poor children. Everyone rushed to remove the twisted mechanism covering the children but found the burden too heavy.

Everyone except Ellen's handler, who ran to her enclosure, unchained her and led her through the frightened crowd. Ellen was as gentle as ever as she lifted the heavy weight and rescued the terrified children. She became an instant celebrity. Everyone wanted to touch her, to stroke her trunk, and thank her for saving those little children. I took special pride in the fact that Ellen had become a personal friend of mine. After all, I had filled her enclosure with shavings from our mill and had walked with her that very morning.

I thought of Ellen's great strength and how she could easily lift the heaviest logs onto the wagons at our mill and it intrigued me. What if we had elephants instead of mules, I mused? Unfortunately, I never saw that gentle giant after that night. The morning after the accident the carnival dismantled, packed up all the tents, rides, and exhibits on the cars of the Great Southern and headed west, its destination said to be somewhere up near Memphis.' Some said they heard Arkansas. I was told a sizeable crowd gathered to see Ellen off and I was saddened to think that I had missed her departure and that I would never see her again.

Chapter Nineteen

Big Timber and Rattlesnakes

Uncle Ernest was hauling a wagon load of logs off the slopes when a large rattlesnake coiled and struck one of his mules. The mules bolted and Ernest lost control of his wagon. He saw the stump but couldn't avoid running over it. The bottom of his wagon brake struck the stump, causing the brake handle to fly forward and strike him hard on the back of his head. As the wagon came bouncing down the mountainside, logs were rolling off and tumbling in all directions. Ernest had been knocked unconscious and he fell from the wagon. Miraculously, no logs rolled over him, but he had been hurt badly. He regained consciousness and, though nauseated, managed to climb back into his wagon. He was extremely disoriented by the time he arrived home. From the mill, we could see him as he reached the cabin. I asked Papa Blackspaniel if I could walk up to the house and check on him. When I arrived, he was slumped in his chair and my aunt was placing a wet towel against a large deformity swelling on the back of his head. My cousins were gathered around him and understandably worried.

"Uncle Ernest, are you okay?" I inquired.

"Yeah, I'll be all right, just need to rest. Better check on my mule, Big Red; I think a snake bit him. I'd check, but I'm sick as a dog and really dizzy right now."

With that, he suddenly heaved across the floor.

"We need a doctor," my aunt cried.

"The nearest one would be at the ironworks. I'll go fetch him."

I hurried outside, unhitched one of the mules, slung my body across his, and dug my heels into his sides. He half ran, half galloped, and as we bounced along, I held on for dear life.

As I rode past Papa and the mill, I called out, "It's Ernest. He's badly hurt. Papa, you need to check on him. I'm headed to the ironworks to get the doctor."

Later, when the doctor and I arrived home, I saw Grandpa and the crew standing solemnly with downcast faces in the yard before the cabin. The mill stood silent. As we grew closer, I could hear my aunt and cousins' pitiful wailing from inside. I had a sickening feeling that fell heavy on my chest. My wonderful uncle was dead. I didn't climb down from the back of my mount; I was too numb and in denial. I sat there and cried my heart out. He had always been so precious to me and everyone, especially his daughters. I didn't think my legs would have supported me if I had dismounted.

Papa sent word to my father that his brother had been killed and he, my mother, siblings, and even my Grandmother O'Mally came down from Grace Mountain. Another millworker rode to Big Grove and notified Grandma Blackspaniel and the family, and by the time they arrived, pine boxes had already been built. Together, we followed an old farm truck with Ernest in his pine box back toward the mountain. We crossed the valley and walked up the mountain to bury our beloved family member. Our procession was slow and somber. Automobiles, wagons, people on horses, and even pedestrians pulled to the side of the road to show respect as we passed. I think all the folks on Big Grove Mountain must have attended Uncle Ernest's wake and funeral. Everyone who knew Uncle Ernest would sadly miss him. He had been a great uncle to me. I will always remember our trip back years ago to Centerville for the saw blade and his laughter while telling of one adventure or another. He was a good man, and we dearly loved him. It seemed that none of us fully recovered from Uncle Ernest's tragic accident. I was devastated and was no longer interested in the timber business. I began to think of other ways to earn a living.

Chapter Twenty
Working on the Chain Gang

Back in 1927, a new road had been proposed for construction across Grace Mountain, and after almost ten years, the Georgia Legislature finally appropriated the funds to begin the grandiose project. As was the custom during this period, Georgia convicts were to be used for much of the labor. My father's sawmill was awarded one of the contracts to furnish lumber for the building of a prison camp in the center of Five Corners, where the workers would live. Most of our neighbors were dead set against it at first, but then the idea of the jobs it would provide in our area outweighed the protests. Our mill near Benge's was winding down, most of the timber was cut, and it was time to move to another location. I opted out of going with them this time, deciding to go to work with my dad at his smaller mill and move back to Grace Mountain and home.

The prison, more appropriately called a prison camp, housed mostly trustees, but there was also a contingent of hardened criminals. The state took advantage of their free labor and sent the men to work on the chain gang to help with much of the construction of the new road. The plan was to pave it using concrete and the road would be the first of its kind anywhere on our mountain. Everyone was excited and eager to drive their new automobiles on it. My father not only would furnish lumber for the prisoners' housing, but he also secured a job for me, driving a state truck, delivering the prisoners to their job sites, and hauling away debris cleared from the route. Many of the convicts were negros and most of them were from South Georgia. I was told the reason for using them was that once they were so far from home, they would be discouraged from running away.

While hauling the prisoners back and forth, I met one old black man who became my favorite. Everyone called him Lucky Joe or more often, just Lucky. Lucky Joe was nearly eighty, a bit of a clown, always laughing and cutting up with me, the guards, and other prisoners. Because of his age and the cool temperatures during the early morning rides to work, I often allowed him to ride in the cab with me and we became friends. Lucky was a hard worker but was easily tired. He was assigned to carry water to the thirsty men, distribute the lunch sacks at noon, and do other menial tasks.

Lucky Joe may have been old but still needed to visit his woman back home, and evidently, she missed him too. It wasn't long until she showed up near Trickum, nearly two hundred long, hard miles from their home in South Georgia. She managed to find employment with a family as their domestic servant down near Trickum.

From time to time, the convicts sing to the rhythmic thump, thump of picks and hammers against a stone. The old convict would quietly slip into the woods and vanish. I knew him to be a reasonably good man whose only crime had been that he had seriously beaten a South Georgia sheriff's deputy who had repeatedly insulted his woman. For that, he got fifteen years of hard labor, which for good behavior was later reduced to minimum labor and trustee status. The first time he disappeared from the so-called chain gang, an all-out manhunt, complete with bloodhounds alerted all the mountain folks that a prisoner was on the loose. It was especially worrisome to the old maids of the community, who would panic for fear of being molested or harmed in some way. Old Joe never bothered anyone of which I was aware. The only sighting of him after his leaving was when he approached a busy neighbor working in his garden. Joe walked to a split rail fence and, leaning against it, asked the gardener for directions off the mountain.

"Sir," he said, "If possible, could you spare just one of dem ripe tomaters and I'll be on my way." The farmer gave him directions, a long drink, and a few tomatoes. Joe politely thanked the man, hurried across a field, and disappeared into the woods.

I was standing outside my work truck when the good Samaritan gardener passed by me a couple of hours later.

"Missing anyone?" he asked apparently amused.

"Yes, as a matter of fact, we are. Lucky Joe. Have you seen him?" I responded.

"I guess that was him who stopped by my farm a few hours ago—seemed harmless enough. I gave him water and food, and he went on his way. You going to report him?" the farmer asked.

"Probably not," I replied. "I'm only a truck driver, not a guard or a warden, and besides, I like the old gentleman."

The state guards initially organized a half-hearted search soon after his disappearance, but that only lasted a couple of days. Then their determination waned, and the search ended. I missed my daily commutes with old Joe riding beside me. He made the workday pass much easier. I missed his teasing and comical antics.

Then, just as he had disappeared, after about a week's absence, he reappeared. Like an apparition, he came walking nonchalantly from the brush as if nothing had happened. He picked up his water bucket and began distributing drinks from the community dipper to the rest of the convicts. I could hear the excitement among his fellow prisoners as they welcomed him back. The guards were happy to see him too but cautioned him not to run off again as it made them look bad to the warden and the state prison system.

"I'se got to have my woman," he would say with a downcast face and a devious grin.

Other prisoners who were sent to our camp were troublemakers. Some were even dangerous, I was told. I interacted with them as little as possible. Any that rode on the bed of my truck were accompanied by an armed guard and followed by another truck carrying additional guards, a large box with bloodhounds, and even a horse trailer with a horse for a mounted deputy.

"You'se needs to watch these men," Lucky Joe would warn. "They's mean uns and will kill you if they needs."

I trusted the old negro and watched the actions of the "mean ones" constantly. I wasn't quite as comfortable driving that truck as I had been earlier. It couldn't have been more than three weeks later that old Joe's prediction came true. Luckily, the anger wasn't directed at me, but at one of the prison guards. Joe and I were at the far end of the work detail, passing the enameled dipper filled with water to thirsty prisoners when a ruckus broke out at the other end of the line. I straightened to see one of the mean ones, a black prisoner named Mulley sprinting from our work project into a dense thicket of woods. Somehow, he had managed to pierce a length of the chain of his leg irons with a heavy pick he was working with in the roadway. After he repeatedly struck the pick against the hard rock where he was working, the chain was severed. A quick lunge with his shoulder knocked the nearest guard into the ditch. I heard one of the guards calling out for him to halt but he dashed on. Another guard shouted again for him to stop, but he continued running. Several shots were fired in his direction, but he entered the trees, obviously unharmed. The dogs, released from their cages, strained at their leashes and barked loudly toward the fleeing man.

The escapee was indeed one of the "meaner ones." His name was John Mulley, but his fellow prisoners called him "Mulehead," a reference to his stubborn, mule-headed attitude. He was serving time for raping his neighbor's wife. He denied the charges, of course, claiming that they had had a mutually agreeable affair. He and his neighbor then had a "knockdown, drag-out" fight where he beat his accuser senselessly and then attacked the wife again and beat her severely. The wife, after recovering, insisted there had been no love affair between them and that John had indeed raped her. No matter now, a Georgia jury had found him guilty, and he was as much a prisoner as the next man working on the chain gang.

As usual, an all-out search ensued. The dogs, straining at their leashes, pulled the guards through the brush frantically to catch up with the desperate man. But Mulehead had a good start, and the dog's leashes were constantly getting entangled in the brush. The clever escapee used a tactic to throw the dogs off to remove his nasty, sweaty prisoner shirt, wrap it around a long stick, and rub it up and down many of the trees he passed. This took only a few seconds but caused the dogs to hesitate at the base of each tree for a few minutes before deciding that the prey was not up in the tree before moving on.

The search for Mulehead ended when the posse reached the banks of a swift mountain stream. With no easy access to cross to the far side, the dogs followed the bank upstream for a couple of hundred yards and then lost the trail. The guards found his state convict shirt tightly wrapped around a stout willow branch extending a few feet into the swiftly flowing creek. Mulehead's scent was constantly being washed into the water downstream which confused the bloodhounds as to where he had crossed the stream.

It wasn't but a day later that a young woman in the mountain community of Harpsville was busy at her wash pot doing her laundry when she was viciously attacked and raped by an unknown assailant. She had also been beaten senseless, as had the woman John Mulley had been convicted of harming earlier. Until she regained consciousness, she could not identify her attacker. Everyone assumed that this young lady was another one of Mulley's victims. Now the whole mountain was on the lookout for the dangerous rapist and a frantic search began.

Two young boys playing nearby found John hiding in an abandoned tool shed near the mountain community of Harpsville. Scared to death, they ran frantically to tell their father. As luck would have it, he was standing in his yard talking to two of the vigilantes. Soon after alerting others searching nearby, a crowd of angry men gathered and surrounded the shed. Calls for Mulehead to give himself up were unsuccessful.

It was a Sunday morning, a day of rest for the prisoners and their guards back at the

SHED WHERE JOHN MULLEY CAPTURED

camp when a man drove up in front of the prison frantically yelling out that John Mulley had been found. About half the guard staff immediately jumped from their seats, grabbed their guns, and rushed to load trucks and drive to the culprit's location. One of the guards took my place in the driver's seat of my car, so I climbed up into the bed, and away we went. They were all desperate to get to the scene, knowing that the crowd would be anxious for revenge. The guard drove like the devil. We bounced over ruts and rocks and slid around curves. I held on for dear life. It wasn't long until we arrived at a scene of pure mayhem. John Mulley had yet to give himself up, and the crowd was reaching a boiling point, a level of anger I had never seen before.

It was believed that John now had possession of some firearm, and no one had dared to storm his hiding place. But the mood of the angry men was growing uglier, and there were calls of simply shooting the shed full of holes or even of piling brush against it and setting it on fire. One of the guards, a man of integrity, called for less violent actions and insisted that attempts be made to talk John out of his hiding place. The angry crowd chose the brush and fire method and quickly began piling armloads of dry brush against the weathered board building. The guard tried to stop the determined vigilantes and pleaded for the men to try to talk Mulehead into giving himself up. I was sickened to my stomach at the thought of burning any man alive.

It wasn't long until the fire burned rapidly against the weathered boards, and the shed became engulfed in flames. It was more than John could stand. He screamed for mercy and burst from the inferno. Several of the men raised their guns to shoot John on sight. He was spared only by the brave and quick action of the guards who rushed to shield him with their own bodies. I was relieved to see that someone in the crowd had the decency of honorable men. Unfortunately, the others, furious at the brazen attack against a white woman by a black convict, had become too full of hatred to turn back now.

The angry mob quickly overpowered the guards, relieved them of their weapons, and took the prisoner away. I watched in disbelief as they tied his hands securely behind his back and then proceeded to punch him unmercifully in the face and head. He was kicked repeatedly and then dragged toward a sturdy oak where a rope had just been tossed over a stout limb. John pleaded again for his life, claiming he had not harmed the woman. Then, I remembered what my Grandfather Blackspaniel had said when I wanted to hang the horse thief. "It's best to wait and learn all the facts before you condemn anyone." Whether

John Mulley was guilty or not, I didn't know, but as they led him to the gallows, I felt sorry for him.

It was my truck they chose to stand him in. They drove it underneath the hangman's noose, lifted John into its bed, and placed the noose securely around his sweaty neck. He was still pleading for mercy. The crowd jeered, laughed, and yelled ugly insults at the panicked man. Then, sadly, the truck was driven from under him. He kicked and jerked and soiled himself in his last desperate struggle. Finally, he swung slightly back and forth while the crowd still roared. A celebration began with men congratulating each other, and several guns were discharged into the swinging corpse. I had just witnessed a man being hanged without a chance to ask for redemption. God forgive us, I thought.

It was three days later when the rape victim regained consciousness. It was then we learned that her assailant had been a white man and not a black person. She identified her assailant as none other than the youngest of the Tisham boys. The community grew quiet. Everyone remained at home, ashamed to show their faces. For weeks afterward, no one dared to mention the lynching and it became eerily quiet around Harpsville. I had been a witness to murder and knew that even if I had tried, I could not have stopped the determined and outraged mob. I was saddened. I returned to my job of driving the prison truck, although my enthusiasm was greatly diminished. Lucky Joe and I stayed friends until one day, he slipped back into the woods, and I never saw him again. I learned later that he had died at home in the company of his loving wife. I would surely miss his joyous soul.

During the time I had worked over on Big Grove Mountain, at Angel's Switch, and then down near Benge, I often wondered what had become of the other Tisham boys and their attractive prices. I knew now that the younger boy had raped the young woman near Harpsville and set in motion the murder of an innocent man. After that, it was rumored that he had fled to Tennessee. The older Tishams, Wash, and Ma, had passed away and were buried in our cemetery at Five Corners across the road from my grandmother's farm. For reasons unknown, something inside me stirred, a good feeling that they would somehow always remain close. I had begun to care for the older Tishams whether I wished to or not.

Chapter Twenty-one
Blue Eyes Lost

By 1938, the construction of the highway across Grace Mountain was complete and several local citizens were now owners of automobiles. My Uncle Tabor O'Mally, in partnership with the peddler Bobo, opened Five Corners' first mercantile store. Uncle Tabor owned and ran the store and Bobo received a percentage for furnishing most of the merchandise. Cousin Otis and little brother June Bug helped Uncle Tabor in the construction of the store. It was a small shot-gun structure offering only the basics but instantly became a favorite hangout for most of the young people on Grace Mountain. Uncle Tabor sold most of the necessities that families needed, but the favorite items were bologna sandwiches, Royal Crown Cola, and Moon Pies. He even boasted the mountain's first gas pump, a tall Sinclair Oil Company model. The girls enjoyed having their pictures taken with it while swinging on the hose. I often saw young ladies dressed in the latest fashions hanging out around the store as if modeling for Sinclair products or possibly Coca-Cola while leaning out of and waving from an open window. The girls were welcome attractions at Uncle's store.

Another of my uncles, Morris O'Mally, recognized the success of Tabor's store and quickly constructed a dam across a small stream immediately across the road from his brother's store. The dam backed up water to create a small lake of about two acres. It provided a perfect swimming hole for the folks lounging near the store to enjoy. He charged an admission fee of a dime on the honor system, which was dropped into an empty tin can nailed to a fence post. He rarely found more than a few cents inside, but he didn't care; he enjoyed watching his nieces and nephews having tons of fun while diving, swimming, and splashing in his new swimming hole. Now, it seemed that the kids of Five Corners enjoyed the attractions offered locally nearly as much as they had the carnival back at Benge years ago.

One Saturday afternoon after swimming, a group of us crossed the road and gathered around our uncle's store to rest and share stories of each other's recent adventures. We were laughing and enjoying the companionship of our friends and neighbors when one of our cousins drove up in a brand-new car. Everyone gathered around, admiring his ride and complimenting him on his choice of models. Eager to prove how powerful the engine was, he invited one of our cousins, a pretty, bosomy blond, to take a ride with him.

Otis nudged me with his elbow and whispered, "If I were her I wouldn't go anywhere with him."

"Why?" I asked.

"You know they're cousins, and he has already taken advantage of her one time. Her parents, being embarrassed, shipped her off to Florida to live with two aunts, and when she returned, there was a baby no one could explain. That's why you haven't seen her around here in over a year. Now that she is back, he will probably try it again."

"I don't believe you!" was all I could say.

"Believe me or not, I don't care. But don't you think it odd that she was gone for months, and soon after she returns, her mother has a baby to care for? Do you remember seeing her mother with a child before her daughter returned from that mysterious vacation?"

I didn't respond. I was dumbfounded as I thought of the possibilities. We watched and waited for her response to his offer to take the ride.

"I would love to, but I'm still wet from swimming," she said longingly.

He grabbed a towel he had brought along and placed it in the passenger seat.

"Come on." he insisted. "We'll run to the county line and come right back. You'll love how fast it will go."

Not willing to resist longer, she jumped into the passenger's seat, and away they sped. She was as obsessed with him as he was with her.

Not knowing if she was placing herself in danger, I quickly called to Otis to jump into my father's truck so that we could follow them. He climbed in and away we went. By the time we topped the first hill, they had already disappeared over the next.

I pushed the pedal down saying, "No way they are going to get away from us."

We sped on. Topping the second rise, we were surprised to see a thick cloud of dust ahead. Quickly applying my brakes, we slowed and came to a stop. Their car had hit a pile of gravel that was scattered across the road, which caused them to veer off the shoulder and hit a pile of sand, which flipped them over. The car rolled for several yards ahead. He was thrown from the wreck but was only shaken. She was still inside the car. Otis and I ran to the wreck and found her unresponsive. We carefully pulled her free and leaned her against the broken automobile. She sat there in an upright posture as though resting. I could find no apparent injuries and yet she had no pulse. It was then I noticed a trickle of blood coming from her mouth and then another from her nostril. We tried to revive her, but all our efforts failed. She was dead. The driver, although dazed, understood that his careless act had killed his beloved cousin, and he grieved pitifully. He was tormented by guilt that he had allowed her to suffer the humiliation of being pregnant and having a child alone while he denied the truth. Afterward, it was rare to see him sober as he was constantly under the influence of moonshine.

    Otis and I loaded the girl into the passenger's seat of my dad's truck. She sat in an upright position and appeared to be resting, as alive as ever. Otis waited with our cousin while I drove her back toward Uncle Tabor's store. Aware that two of her brothers were waiting, I pulled off the highway and parked a few yards shy of the store. I wanted to inform them of the tragic accident before bringing her lifeless body back there. It was another of the saddest days of my young life as she had been one of our favorite of our cousins.

    Both of the youths involved were not only kinfolks but were inseparable friends. The driver declared his intention to kill himself, which reminded almost everyone of the earlier threat and execution by poor Mr. Biddle after the death of his daughter. Almost everyone pleaded that he reconsider, and her father, although devastated, intervened, explaining that his actions had been foolish but to lose two lives would be too hard on the community. Her father never realized that the driver was the same person who had impregnated his daughter. That father's forgiveness further strengthened my faith in people's caring for others; however, I wondered if I could have found that much forgiveness in me. My cousin's funeral and burial were held at the old Methodist Church and the cemetery only a hundred yards or so from the pond where she had enjoyed her last day on earth swimming with her family and friends.

Now, once again my thoughts returned to how much I missed Willow. I borrowed my father's pickup, bought three dollars worth of gas at Uncle Tabor's store, and drove off the mountain toward Trickum then north to Angel's Switch. I imagined finding her working in her uncle's store and dressed in one of the pretty cotton dresses that always accentuated her natural radiance.

Arriving in front of the store, I stepped out of my father's truck, straightened my pants, and walked into the store as nonchalantly as possible. As I had expected, she was behind the counter, but less radiant than I had remembered. She looked up from her work, silent and unmoved, with her mouth slightly open.

"Hello Willow," I said as politely as possible.

"Danny," she answered, her voice nervous. "I thought I would never see you again."

"I know; we've been busy at the sawmill lately."

"Too busy to come by just to say hello?"

I could see tears filling her eyes.

"You promised to write."

"I'm sorry Willow, but I did write many times."

"No, you didn't, and you'll never make it up," she said sternly. "I'm married now!"

My knees almost buckled and I leaned on the counter with my mouth gaping open.

"What?" I said in disbelief.

"Yes, I married Francois from down at the train depot. And with Mom and Dad's blessings, too," she said sarcastically.

Stunned and embarrassed, I straightened and tried to regain my composure. I didn't know how to react. I had come to wish her well and find out why my letters were never answered but I never expected this. Now I was more confused than ever.

"Please don't tell me you're married. Please be kidding," I begged.

"Not only am I married but I am with child."

My legs weakened further and I slumped into the nearest chair.

"Daniel, you never came back, you never wrote. Not one time like you promised."

"Willow, I wrote to you dozens of times and waited for you to write me back."

"I never received the first letter from you. I'm sorry, but I'm married now."

I choked back my tears in disbelief. I was totally confused and lost. All I could think to say was,

"Willow, I am sorry for being such a jerk. I don't understand. I wish you and Francois all the best." I stumbled through the door.

I was devastated and saddened to have missed my chance for true love. Stunned and grieving, I climbed back into my dad's truck and drove away from that little country store with tears streaming down my face.

Chapter Twenty-two

Chicago or Bust

It was with a broken heart, or at least one that was permanently damaged, that I decided to give up on love and submerge myself in the unknown of the open road once again. This time I chose to travel to the great Midwest and the big city of Chicago. I had seen a copy of a letter written to my cousin Bobby Joe from his uncle who had traveled much of the United States looking for work. He found employment in the Chicago suburb of Calumet City and was now encouraging all his friends to come to Chicago to find work. A copy of the letter had been posted in the window of the mercantile in Trickum and as a result, several local men had packed their bags and headed there. Bobby Joe had already gone and had written home with glowing letters of all the "really great" job opportunities. It sounded good to me. I knew I could stay with him and his uncle for a while, and I was ready for a change. Sawing timber was hard work, and my hands had become worn and calloused. This time, I informed my parents of my intentions, and knowing that Bobby Joe would watch out for me, they wished me luck and gave me their blessing. I packed a valise with clean socks and underwear, a couple of shirts, pants, and overalls for when I found work. I had a small pistol in my pocket but not the bottle of whiskey that my grandfather was known for. I also had ten dollars in my billfold and another twenty-dollar bill folded and secretly hidden inside the toe of my shoe.

I cut a fair-sized piece of cardboard from an old box and carefully printed the message, "Chicago or Bust." I caught my first ride off the mountain with a neighbor who was going as far as Trickum. From there I pointed my thumb into the air and enthusiastically began my trip toward the famous Windy City. My travels took me through Angel's Switch, and I tried not to think of my dear Willow. I was much too heartbroken. I passed through Centerville and continued northwest toward the Cumberland Mountains. Late on the first evening, my ride ended in a narrow valley and I could see the tall, imposing mountains rising from the valley floor ahead of me. As I was let off, the driver told me I would have to cross over that obstacle. He turned his vehicle up a secluded country lane and disappeared into the distance.

Then, I walked along the highway alone. There was not much traffic this late and the area looked foreboding. I was faced with the prospect of sleeping on the ground and to be honest, this was a most inhospitable-appearing valley. It got worse, and as night fast approached I found myself standing at the edge of the highway and looking across the road into the entrance of a gaping cavern with a stream of water flowing from its entrance. Beautiful I thought at first, but at the same time kind of spooky because of the remoteness of the area. Thinking I could possibly find a safer place up the road, I hurried on another half mile and saw to my left a small church. The sign above the door said, "Cavern Springs Baptist Church." I thought it odd that I had not seen any residences anywhere nearby to support this secluded place of worship. But now it was growing late, and the air was fluttering with bats coming from the roof of the cavern. Considering the seclusion, the darting bats, and the darkening sky, I became concerned for my safety.

I stood in the churchyard and wondered if the building could provide a safe place to spend the night. An unexpected flash of light illuminated the sky over the mountain, and I immediately climbed the steps and stood, considering whether I should try to enter. A second flash, and after a short pause, the distant rumbling of thunder assured me I needed shelter. I tried the church door and, to my surprise, found it unlocked. I opened it and, leaning in, I called out, "Hello, anyone here?" I didn't expect an answer. No one should be here on a weeknight. I eased into the darkness and walked to the nearest pew. I placed my valise in the seat for a pillow, stretched out, and drifted off to sleep. I vaguely remembered turning occasionally to relieve the aches and pains from lying on the hard oak pews. I was reminded of the night spent with Uncle Ernest and Grandpa when we slept in the wagon bed when his horse was "borrowed." The following day, I was awakened by whispering. Startled, I quickly rose to a sitting position. Standing in front of me was a man and two small children.

They were just standing there, looking at me with an expression as if looking at some museum exhibit.

"Morning," the gentleman said with a reassuring smile.

"Good morning," I replied, as I tried to rise to my feet. My bones ached from a night of sleeping on that pew.

"Welcome to the Cavern Springs Baptist Church. I'm Benjamin Worley the pastor here, and these are my sons," he said.

"My name is Samuel Blackspaniel," I replied. "I'm sorry for the intrusion but I was concerned with the lightning and the rain last night."

"No worries. It did pour, didn't it? I wouldn't expect anyone to sleep out there in the dampness."

"And besides," the pastor continued, "plenty of other travelers have sought shelter here and they are always welcome. Just wish more would return on Sunday morning."

"Thank you, sir. I'd better get moving. Gotta climb that mountain up yonder. It's a long trip to Chicago."

I gathered my things, bade the preacher and his son farewell, and walked away from the little church. Rides came often through that stretch of Tennessee. By the evening of the third day, I had reached the little community of Providence, a few miles south of Hopkinsville, Kentucky. Walking north, out of Providence, a gentleman slowed, pulled to the side of the road and waited while I ran briskly to his car.

"Howdy there, young fellow," he greeted me as I slid into the passenger seat. "Going to Chicago, I see from your sign. You live up there?"

"No sir, going there to see if I can find work," I answered.

"Names Frank, Frank Croxton," he said, extending his hand,

"It is good to meet you, Mr. Croxton. I sure appreciate the ride," I said, shaking his hand.

"What kind of work do you do?" He asked.

"I've been a truck driver and have driven for the state of Georgia. Before that, I worked in the timber industry," I said boastfully.

"Humm," he said thoughtfully, probably wondering how many of my claims were accurate. I was still a young man in my teens. "I guess there's lots of truck driving jobs there. Jobs in timber would probably be further north, possibly in Wisconsin or Minnesota."

He continued, "Most of my time in the woods has been spent searching for and digging ginseng. It brings a decent profit nowadays if you can find it."

"Ginseng?" I thought, remembering that it was a favorite occupation of a few of the old-timers back on Grace Mountain. I had hunted it a couple of times with my O'Mally uncles but had little success.

"It is a root," he continued. "A tubular, similar to a crooked carrot usually with two smaller legs. A herb old folks and healers use for curing insomnia, impotence, hemorrhaging, and such."

"Wow!" I had no idea what any of those words meant. And I was still trying to picture a carrot with two legs.

"I've found as much as ten dollars' worth in just a couple of weekends," he continued.

Now my interest was piqued. Ten dollars for a couple of weekends.

"And you find it while roaming around in these woods?" Sounded to me like he had found a hidden treasure.

We rode along quietly for a while. I was thinking, visualizing being in the woods looking for a plant worth its weight in gold.

"Is it true that all you have to do is go into these woods and dig up a root, and someone will pay you all that money for it?" I asked.

He grinned and said, "Well, it's not all that easy, but it is there, deep within the thick growth of trees. Hunting for it is more of a hobby than a job. I look for honey, too. Wild honey is found in the recesses of hollow trees. Bees are plentiful across this landscape if you know where to look."

I looked at him, studying his features as we rode along. He seemed honest enough and sincere, and I guessed he was telling me the truth. I searched the landscape as it passed beside us as we drove north. I imagined thick patches of ginseng scattered everywhere under the canopy of the trees. Any semblance of mountains had disappeared back in Tennessee. We were in Kentucky now, and the landscape was flat, with gently rolling hills and thick woods.

"It's getting late now," he said. "Come home with me and spend the night. You must be hungry, and you could use a bath."

My host quickly reminded me of the ride I had accepted with the Black youths back in Georgia on my trip to Brazil. I glanced toward him, embarrassed, but his smile was reassuring and forgiving.

He said, "My wife, Bonnie, will have supper ready, and after we eat, you can bathe. I'll help her get your bed ready. It belonged to my brother-in-law, her brother, who recently joined the Navy. He shipped out about a month ago, and we've been busy packing his stuff up for storage, but right now, it is still piled on his bed. It shouldn't take long to remove, and you should be comfortable there.

I liked Mr. Croxton almost from the beginning. After about thirty minutes, we pulled into the driveway of his home in Fairview, Kentucky. In the last rays of the setting sun, I could see a tall monument standing in the distance.

"What is that?" I asked, pointing in its direction.

"Oh, that is a monument to the President of the Confederacy, Jefferson Davis. He was born there. The obelisk is three hundred and fifty feet tall. If you get lost around here, just use it as your guide," he laughed.

After bathing, I joined Frank and Bonnie for dinner. She was a fine cook and an excellent conversationalist. I enjoyed listening to the stories of her family and the histories of the places scattered across that part of the country. After dinner, Frank led me to his barn, where he had layers of ginseng root drying on bed sheets.

"Well, this is ginseng he said," watching for my reaction.

He handed me a handful of the dried, fleshy roots. They were as light as feathers. If these are worth their weight in gold, how many wheelbarrow loads would it take to make a profit? It would require long hours of searching and digging through the woods. Still, I wondered how anyone could make a profit of ten dollars for just two weekends of work.

"Tell you what," he said. Why don't you plan to stop by here if you change your mind about Chicago? I'll teach you how to find ginseng and locate honey bees?"

Odd hobbies, I thought, saying, "If I'm back this way, I'll be sure to stop by."

Rising early the following day, I found Bonnie busy preparing breakfast, and Frank was returning from their barn with a basket of fresh eggs. I washed up and joined them at the table. Frank asked for God's blessings, and we discussed what we could do together if I returned one day. After thanking them, Frank took me back to the main highway and handed me a sack lunch Bonnie had prepared. Turning north, I put my thumb out and walked along as trucks and cars sped by, blasting me with air. Most of the morning, my attempts at catching a ride were fruitless, and then a heavy truck hauling freight pulled to the side of the road and waited.

I climbed into the cab, exchanged pleasantries, and rode through the evening and into the night. When I woke the following day, we were on the outskirts of Terre Haute, Indiana, the trucker's final destination.

"Young man, this is as far as I go. You still have about a hundred and eighty miles to Chicago, but it's pretty much a straight shot from here. All the best to you. Be safe."

I climbed down from the truck, stretching my arms, yawning, and looked around. I needed a cup of coffee and a couple of eggs, but otherwise, I was well-rested. And eager to get started. I continued my travels toward Chicago by eating in a small diner on the main route through the city. It wasn't long until another freight truck stopped and offered me a ride.

"You the guy going to Chicago?" the driver surprised me by asking.

"Yes sir, how did you know?

"My buddy gave you the ride to Terre Haute. He said I should watch for you."

"How far are you going?" I asked.

"All the way. I have a delivery in Calumet City."

"Calumet City? That's where my cousin lives." I said in astonishment.

We rode along together with minimum conversation. This driver wasn't much of a talker. I watched as miles of flat terrain spread past my window. I was astonished by the absence of any mountains. Surely, growing up here was boring.

Arriving at the outskirts of Calumet City, I quickly found a phone booth, looked it up, and dialed Bobby Joe's number. A sleepy voice answered, "Hello."

"Is this Bobby Joe? This is Boogie. I'm here, buddy."

He asked me where I was, and I told him at the corner of Pulaski Road and Wentworth Avenue.

"Hold on, wait right there, and I'll be there shortly," he said. "Give me about twenty minutes. I need to get my pants on."

It was obvious that I had awakened him from his sleep, but it was the middle of the afternoon, I thought. I waited for about thirty minutes and then I heard the "hooga-hooga" of a horn. Looking in that direction I saw my cousin waving wildly. He had the biggest smile on his face.

"Dadburn, it's Boogie, you made it. You're here."

I felt a sense of accomplishment. Traveling from Grace Mountain to Chicago was a big deal to me.

Bobby Joe was driving a spiffy new 1932 Ford Roadster, which caught my attention at once. However, probably more concerning to me was the fact that he had a pronounced accent. I could hardly understand him.

"Where did you learn to talk like that?"

"Oh, that's the way they talk up here. I was told it's called Blaacent. It's how Chicagoans speak, kind of like a Northeastern Yankee accent."

"The last two truck drivers I had ridden with spoke with the same accents, but they grew up here. I'm surprised to hear you talk that way."

I had not expected my southern cousin to be sounding like a foreigner.

"What do you think of my new ride?" he asked.

"I love it. You must be doing well up here."

"Yep, doing okay. I'm the night attendant of an all-night service station at Wentworth and State Street. I've already asked my boss if I could hire you as my assistant and he said yes, we needed somebody. It's a busy little place at night."

"Oh, you see that bank up there?" he said, pointing in its direction. "They say that the famous Al Capone robbed it a few years back."

"Wow," I said, rising in my seat for a better look. "The real Al Capone?"

"Sure, lots of gangsters up here. Some even hang out at our station some nights. Of course, so do a lot of police officers. It seems they are all friends to some degree. Most grew up in the same neighborhoods. Boogie, you'll love Chicago. It's a rip-roaring town."

But gangsters, I thought. The idea scared me. I remembered the infamous massacre of 1929.

We drove north on Wentworth to the intersection of State Street, and Bobby Joe pointed to the service station where he worked.

"Five pumps," he said. "We stay busy at night."

Then he turned north onto State Street. It wasn't long until I had my first real experience of the legendary Windy City. I was shocked and embarrassed to see open burlesque in full bloom on the street. Loud music boomed from bars and speakeasies, and near-naked girls danced freely just inside wide-opened doors. Hawkers stood outside and invited you in to see risqué shows. I had never seen anything like it before and didn't know how to react. Chicago was not Five Corners. It wasn't long until Bobby Joe pulled into the driveway of a large two-story house.

"This is it," he said. "Uncle and I rent the downstairs apartment. A Polish family lives upstairs, but they pretty much stay to themselves."

We entered the house from a side door into the kitchen, and Bobby Joe opened the ice box and handed me a beer. I motioned it away.

"No, thank you. I haven't learned to like beer yet."

"What are you, Boogie, a communist?" he said jokingly.

I wasn't sure if I should be offended or not. I didn't know what a communist was.

We talked for a while, and then he said. "You better get some rest, Boogie. It'll be a long night if you don't."

He removed some clutter from the couch, handed me a pillow and blanket, and said, "The couch will be your bed until we can arrange for something else. Now get some sleep, and I'll wake you when it's time."

I tried to sleep but was too excited about being in Chicago to rest. Then, Bobby Joe stood over me, shaking my arm, and I was awakened from a deep slumber.

"Wake up Boogie, it's time to rise and shine. It's time to go to work."

As we readied to leave, his uncle came in. I didn't know him that well as he was Bobby Joe's uncle on his mother's side.

"Hey Daniel," he said. "Welcome to Chicago."

Bobby said that his uncle worked at one of Chicago's meat-packing plants and that he had tried it in the beginning but found the odors of carcasses nauseating. Filling tanks with gas and topping off oil at the service station was far more pleasant.

We loaded into Bobby's roadster and drove to the station where I would begin my first night of work. Remembering again what Bobby Joe said about gangsters hanging out there made me nervous. Bobby Joe had me follow him to watch and learn as customers came into the station and asked for different amounts of gas. After filling their orders, he would lift their hoods, pull out the oil stick, remove a rag from his back pocket, and wipe the stick clean. Then he would insert it back into the oil, and quickly remove it to see if they needed any oil. He also quickly sprayed their bug-riddled windshields and, with a second rag, cleaned away any debris. His business was a full-service station. A palace of a station compared to anything we had back at Trickum. I thought being an attendant here was a simple enough procedure, and I was soon handling many of the customers myself.

It was about midnight when several policemen came into the station. I learned that after making the first of their routine patrols, the service station was their hangout. I had not expected the jovial camaraderie of these men. Almost every night, just before midnight, Billy Joe called their favorite pizza parlor and ordered four large pepperoni pies. All the participants pitched in a set amount, which included the cost of the pizzas and a small tip for the delivery guy. He was as much a part of the crowd as the rest and usually remained and ate one or two slices along with the other fellows. I waved off any part of the cost since I didn't eat pizza. I had never tasted what appeared to be a tomato pie and was sure I wouldn't like it. My dinner on that first night consisted of candy bars and a soda pop. The cops, my cousin, and a few other late-night regulars laughed, teased, and ate pizza well into the night. The cops always had entertaining stories of those they had chased and arrested. I was proud to be included in their circle of friends.

All during the night the radios in their police cars rattled off reports of possible crimes being committed in the different areas around Calumet City. Most calls, however, were for drunken altercations up and down State Street. The cops would run to their cars, still eating the last slices of pizza, and roll away from the service station with sirens whining loudly. Usually, within minutes they would pull back onto the lot with another humorous story of some character's misfortune.

It was thought that Bobby Joe's 1932 Ford was one of the fastest cars in Chicago. It boasted one of the new V8 engines, and he was constantly working on it in his spare time. Working in a service station provided access to all the tools and latest technology necessary to soup up his car. His friends and the local police often encouraged his wild street antics like laying rubber or revving up the motor to hear the engine roar to gain the attention of cute girls on the sidewalks. Bobby Joe was cool, and I was his smug-acting cousin. He and I would ride around on the streets with the top down. Our arms dangling from open windows, and our shirtsleeves rolled up tight to reveal our arm muscles that we didn't really have. Under our stylish hats, we wore our hair greased back tightly to our heads. Man! We were both so cool. I even felt slightly akin to the gangster element I hadn't experienced yet.

As fate would have it, a couple came by the station later that week.

Bobby Joe sidled up beside me, nodded in their direction, and whispered, "Those two are part of the racketeers that I told you to come by occasionally. They will fill up their tank, tell you to put it on their tab and drive off. They never pay for gas, cigarettes, or anything, but our owner considers it a small price to pay to remain in their favor. Thugs from other gangs ignore us for fear of reprisals if they harm us. "

I saw nothing that would make me think of a gangster. They were clean-shaven, nicely groomed, and dressed in the most stylish suits and fedoras. It was their manners that betrayed them. They proved to be arrogant, pushy, and demanding. Bobby Joe was accustomed to their snide remarks, and they were pleasant enough with him, but I remained suspicious and uncomfortable. It wasn't long until I was told that they were owners of two of the speakeasies on State Street. Being a simple country boy and unaccustomed to women dancing half-naked for all the world to see made me extremely uneasy, and I didn't know how to react. I was at a loss when they offered Bobby Joe and me free passes for a show.

"Bobby Joe, I can't be going to a burlesque show; my mama would kill me," I complained.

"Boogie, your mama ain't never going to know. Besides, you don't want to offend either of these two guys. Sooner or later, they'll return to the station, and you know they'll ask how you enjoyed the show."

It seemed I was caught between a rock and a hard place. Thinking about it, I realized it was kind of exciting to be the guest of the owners, even if they were gangsters. Kind of made you feel special. And then I remembered the doctor who wanted to be associated with the gangsters who were murdered during the infamous St. Valentine's Day Massacre.

"Bobby, I can't go. I have no jacket. Don't they require a jacket to get in?"

"I'll loan you a jacket; now quit fretting about it. You're going, and that's all there is to it."

Our boss really couldn't spare Bobby Joe on either a Friday or Saturday night but also felt that he shouldn't offend either of the hoodlums. He had us replaced on Friday night by a couple of old cronies and my cousin and I spiffed up, spit-shined and polished. The coat Bobby Joe loaned me was at least two sizes too big, but at least I qualified to pass by the doorman. I'll never forget that night. We arrived in style in Bobby's roadster and were allowed to park near the entrance to the club. I already felt special. I followed Bobby Joe as we were allowed to "buck" the line of others waiting eagerly for admission. We were like gangsters ourselves. We discreetly presented our passes, and the bouncers greeted us cordially and motioned us in. I noticed that, once inside, our celebrity status greatly diminished. We were seated toward the back of the room and away from the stage where the girls danced. Our waiter seemed quite annoyed when Bobby ordered a whiskey and I ordered a soda. There wasn't much profit in a soda. With all the moonshine made on Grace Mountain, I still had never acquired the taste for alcohol.

I was aware that I was not an ideal customer like many of the others who were willing to spend most of their paychecks on booze. I expected that the entertainment would be provided by the half-naked girls I had seen when passing the open doors of the other joints on State Street. Instead, the majority of the show was provided by a comedian who I found corny, but slightly funny. I listened to his setups and the following punch lines, and as the drunken crowd got caught up in the laughter, I found myself laughing as well.

I was soon enjoying the gaiety of the evening. It seemed everyone was having a good time. Everyone was drinking, laughing, and getting louder and louder. Cousin Bobby Joe fit right in as he joined in the conversations with the few folks he knew from his work at the station. My attention was drawn to an exceptionally pretty girl who came in with several other people. Our eyes met almost instantly, and she smiled. I formed a "Wow" on my lips, which she seemed to understand. She smiled again and sat at a table with her friends, still looking in my direction.

Between the acts of the girls dancing and the comedian telling his corny jokes, the house band played music, and the drunken patrons danced. I watched as the girl I had been attracted to danced with a couple of different guys that she had entered the club with. I was nothing more than a clumsy country boy, but I sure did want to dance with that pretty girl. Finally gaining enough courage, I walked to her table and asked if she would dance with me. She slid easily from her seat and took my hand and led me to the floor.

"What's your name?" I asked.

"Arlene, and yours?"

"Daniel, Daniel Blackspaniel." I answered.

"You're not from around here, are you?" she teased.

"Nope, I'm from Grace Mountain down in Georgia.

"My goodness, you are a long way from home, aren't you?"

The band finished their song and I led Arlene back to her table. As she walked past one of the young men in their group, he caught her arm and pulled her onto his lap. I could see he was drunk, but I could also see that Arlene was not protesting. She placed her arms around his neck and kissed him on his cheek. He whispered something into her ear, and from that moment on, she completely ignored me. I was well aware that I was a terrible dancer but surely I deserved an explanation. I was mustering the courage to invite her to dance again when another young man staggered to her table and asked her instead. As she attempted to rise from the first guy's lap, he grabbed her and pulled her down again. Then an argument broke out. I couldn't understand what was being said, but both were loud and cursing at each other. Suddenly, the first youth shoved the young lady from his lap, jumped up, and drew a small pistol from his pocket. "Bam!" He shot the other poor fellow, the bullet striking him in the top of his forehead. The bouncers at once jumped the shooter, wrestled the gun from his hands, and began to give him a good pummeling. I had seen gunfights before, remembering the shootout at the Tishams, but this scared me. I realized that I could have been the victim. As they escorted the shooter past me, I noticed his front teeth were missing; the bouncers had knocked them out. He looked at me with the hardest expression and mumbled something like, "I'll be seeing you, too."

More astonishing, however, was the discovery that the victim was still alive. I heard him moan and then he grabbed his forehead and began to roll around on the floor in pain. The bullet had been a glancing blow. I struggled to help him to his feet, and it was then I noticed a sizable notch missing from his left ear. Stunned, I realized I was helping none other than Doolittle Tisham to stand. Still groggy and with blood streaming down his face, he didn't recognize me. Shocked, I thought it was impossible that I could come to Chicago and run smack dab into an old adversary. The chances must have been a million to one. Bobby Joe reminded me that several fellows from our area had responded to his uncle's letter encouraging men from Grace Mountain to come to Chicago for work, and apparently, the Tishams were no exception. They had also answered the request and drifted to the windy city looking for jobs or simply to escape justice for the killing of the deputies and the sheriff and his jailer.

Running into one of the Tisham boys this far from home ended my enthusiasm for Chicago. I realized then that I would probably be a lot safer back on Grace Mountain and decided to return home. I suggested to Bobby Joe that he should consider coming with me. He said he would take his chances; he liked Chicago and had lots of police friends to protect him. He would report our discovery to the local authorities and allow them to handle the Tishams.

Later that night back at the apartment, I told Bobby Joe and his uncle of my plan to return to Georgia. I was never comfortable being so far from home anyway. As I packed my valise, I realized I had saved enough money to buy a bus ticket back to Centerville. But then I would have none left for my mother or for the necessities of living on my own again. I had hitchhiked north to Illinois, and I could hitchhike back to Georgia. I resigned myself to the fact that I would probably end up again at one of the sawmills on either Grace or Big Grove Mountain.

The following morning, I was up early and preparing to leave. Bobby's uncle had already left for work. I removed a bottle of milk from the ice box and poured myself a half glass since the bottle was almost empty. As I drank, Bobby Joe came into the kitchen dressed in his undershorts and tee shirt.

"So, you're heading back to Georgia are you, Boogie?"

"Sure, there's nothing for me here, and I miss my family," I answered.

"We have enjoyed your visit Boogie, and I hate to see you go." Bobby Joe said sadly. "Let me get dressed and I'll run you out to the main highway headed south.

I was sad to be leaving but eager to head toward home. The wind blew cool in my face as I rode in that beautiful, red roadster for the last time. Bobby Joe pulled to the curb at the intersection of State Street and U.S. Hwy. 41. We bade each other a fond farewell, and he roared off back toward Calumet City. I stuck my thumb out and began the long trek toward home. To my surprise, I was at once picked up by a trucker headed south. He was hauling a load of packaged meat to a large distribution center near Memphis, and I thought that a satisfactory direction since it was in Tennessee. We talked little as he drove the highway south, and soon, all grew quiet, and I dozed off to the gentle - back-and-forth rocking of the big truck. I awakened as he slowed for a rest stop near Cairo, Illinois, and I learned that we had traveled on Illinois Route 37 and had long since left U. S. Highway 41 behind. My planned visit with Mr. Croxton and his wife Bonnie was dashed for now. The driver handed me a blanket for warmth, removed a pillow and another blanket for himself, and curled up to sleep for the night. I wrapped myself in my blanket, rolled my coat for a pillow and we both drifted off for a good night's rest.

He had parked in a large lot that had a gas station and a small restaurant. Early the next morning, I awakened as he pulled to the pumps to fuel, and then we walked to the restaurant for breakfast. I offered to pay our tab, but the driver refused, saying he would get his and I should get mine. He thought I should use my money for greater needs. That afternoon, as we approached Memphis, he asked me where I wanted off. I asked for any road toward northwest Georgia, and he said that U. S. Highway 72 was probably my best bet. He let me off, and I obtained directions to the beginning of Highway 72. When I finally reached it, I found rides few and far between. I ended up walking five or six miles before my first one.

My rides along Highway 72 were usually short, often no more than five to ten miles, and the further I found myself from Memphis, the more secluded the route became. As evening approached, I found myself now in Mississippi, the middle of nowhere, walking in light rain and in need of shelter. It was cool and a mist began to settle in the recesses of every depression. It was spooky being here alone and so far from home. Finally, as the last light of day faded, I spotted the remnants of an abandoned barn. It sat off a distance from the highway and was shrouded in a ghostly fog which made it far more daunting than it probably was. I threaded through patches of weeds and briers as I worked toward the shelter.

This one was much spookier than any visited by my friend Johnny Smothers and me when on our travels to Brazil. I wasn't as brave when approaching this ancient structure as I had been with Johnny. I couldn't see any farmhouse nearby, and this barn was in shambles but surely would offer some protection from the rain. I approached cautiously, listening for any sounds from inside. The door hung haphazardly on one hinge, and it squeaked eerily as I eased it open. The stalls had been vacant for a long while and the rungs of the ladder to the loft were broken or missing. I lifted myself with the help of beams and walked slowly across the loft boards, testing each cautiously as I made my way to a corner of the room where a few old sacks lay abandoned. They were dusty and smelled of mildew. I shook them briskly, and suddenly, a large owl whose daily roost was on a rafter above me hooted loudly and flew swiftly past me, brushing me with its outstretched wing as it flew away. I yelled like a little girl and almost had a heart attack. After settling down, I felt silly and was glad no one was around to see my cowardice.

The night air was growing colder, and a myriad of cracks between the boards allowed a breeze to pass freely through the loft. I was thankful to have the ragged sacks to cover my body in an attempt to keep warm. I was pretty exhausted but was unable to either rest or sleep. I had barely laid my head down when I heard that old barn door creak. Was someone else entering the barn? I lay perfectly still and listened. There was an occasional thump or bump in the hall below me, and I knew I was not alone. I continued to remain still and listen. After a time, because of my exhaustion, I would start to doze, and then I would hear another bump. I even imagined I could hear someone quietly climbing up the ladder to the loft where I lay in panic. The thumps and bumps lasted through the night and I expected any time to be pounced upon by an unknown assailant.

It's funny what one's imagination can conjure up. I lay awake all during the night exhausted while having visions of other vagabonds prowling about or even a ghost or some ferocious beast climbing up to pounce on me. I was afraid to move from my cover of sacks until finally, it was light enough outside to see. I moved cautiously from my place in the loft to find the source of my torment. While easing across that aged loft, I accidentally stepped on a creaking board, and suddenly, a family of raccoons fled from the hallway where they had been playing and scampered off into the early morning mist. I gathered my composure and, although slightly embarrassed, I walked away from that ghostly apparition which was still shrouded in mist. I thought of what my Grandpa Blackspaniel would have said. "Daniel, before making a judgement wait until you have all the facts."

I had not walked far on Hwy. 72 until I saw a large delivery truck rolling toward me and heading east. I stuck my thumbs into the air, and it slowed and stopped a few yards ahead of me. I ran to where it was, and after thanking the driver for stopping, I asked how far he was going.

"Huntsville," he said, "I'm going to Huntsville."

I smiled, leaned against my valise to rest, and woke occasionally as he slowed to pass through some small village or town.

"Young fellow," he said as he shook my arm, "I'm stopping here to fuel and get a bite to eat. You hungry?"

"Yes sir, I am," I said groggily.

While the station attendants filled his tank, we walked to the restrooms to wash up and then to the restaurant for lunch. We were now somewhere in Alabama and within a few miles of Huntsville. Within a couple more days I should be at home on Grace Mountain or at least as close as Big Grove. The country that I traveled through now was far different from back in Calumet City near Chicago. I was enjoying the sounds of the South, the distinct Southern drawl of the folks around me, and even the distinct songs of the sparrows in the trees. I shut my eyes and smiled, content to be nearing home again.

On returning to my beloved Grace Mountain, I found the place and its residents little changed. If anything, jobs were fewer and every family worked at what they could find. I asked my father if he could use me at the sawmill, and he gave me a job as an off-bearer, one who tosses the slabs sawed from fresh logs onto the burn pile. Being an off-bearer is hard work, made harder from constantly breathing sawdust and smoke as we burned the slab pile, but it was honest work, and there were no gangsters around. The Tishams were still somewhere up in Chicago.

It wasn't long until we learned that the shooting victim up in Chicago had been positively identified as Doolittle Tisham. Billy Joe immediately informed his police buddies that the Tishams were wanted back in Georgia for the murders of a sheriff and several deputies. Once again, the authorities moved too slowly and made a botched attempt at capturing them. They did manage to capture Edgar, the oldest of the brothers. They said he made no attempt to flee and gave up without a struggle, saying he was tired of running and wanted to pay for everything he had done. Doyle and Doolittle managed to elude capture and eventually made their way back to Grace Mountain. When word got around that they were back, they took on a kind of undeserved celebrity status. They openly flaunted the law, claiming they could not be captured. It seemed they had forgotten the determination of the new sheriff, John Graham Hiram. Learning of their return, he made no fuss and pretended to care less about the presence of the Tisham gang.

Edgar was extradited to Georgia, stood trial, and was found guilty. However, he humbled himself and freely admitted to his part in the Tishams' past crimes. Surprisingly, he was sentenced to only eighteen years of hard labor, which astonished everyone considering the seriousness of his crimes. Most thought it far too lenient. Possibly, someone remembered that one of the deputies had slapped his mother.

Chapter Twenty-three

Slabs or Shine

Life went on as usual at our sawmill. Early one morning, as we began work, a large, flatbed truck with high sideboards slowly entered our mill yard. An older gentleman, bent with age, slowly climbed down from the cab and walked to where I stood, throwing slabs onto a pile for burning.

"Howdy," he greeted me as he approached me, walking with the aid of a cane. "Was wondering if I could buy some of these slabs? Folks around here could use them to burn for heat this coming winter." I recognized him as none other than Marmaduke MacKurdy. He looked older and more fragile, but it was him, and he was still driving that old, rattling pickup.

"You'll need to check with my boss. He's the man running the saw over there." I replied. He limped gingerly toward my father who shut the mill down to hear the old man's inquiry better.

"Well, hello, Marmaduke," I heard my dad say. "What brings you to Grace Mountain?"

"Howdy," he repeated. "Wondered if one could buy some of them slabs to use as fuel for winter heat? Lots of folks around here could use them but have no way to haul them, so it occurred to me that since I have this old truck and spare time, I could haul them and make a little extra money."

My father smiled and said, "Mister, you get all you want. We already have a few people who come by regularly and haul off a load, and what they don't get, we usually burn when the pile gets too high. You just come by as you need and load all you want."

The old man smiled and asked if he could get a load today.

"Just back your truck up right there, and as we see them off, we will pitch them on the truck for you," my dad told him.

He eagerly backed his truck into place, and we filling his truck. While I loaded the slabs coming from the sawmill, he collected others from our slab pile and we soon had his truck heavily loaded.

"How much do I owe you?" he inquired.

"Not a penny," my father answered. "Lots of folks around here can use your service and as long as you deliver our slabs for a fair price you can have them for the hauling."

He thanked my father and, with an extra big smile, drove away.

As the weeks passed and the weather cooled toward winter, he returned again and again for more loads of slabs. He was doing well with his firewood delivery business. I often saw him passing on the country roads, always driving slowly, being extra cautious with his overly burdened truck.

"No chance the law will stop him for reckless driving I thought."

In fact, he drove so slowly that he was considered a nuisance when folks in a hurry were forced to follow him up some twisted mountain road. If someone complained, he would counter by saying, "That if they were in such a hurry to get somewhere, they should have gotten up and left home earlier." I was astonished each time I met him, usually in the most unexpected places. He was always busy making his deliveries to the remotest of families, and it seemed that most of them appreciated his service. I started to envy him somewhat. He had found a way to make a little money and I wondered why I had never thought of it. Maybe I could deliver coal. Coal was what the "better off" families burned. It burned hotter than the cheaper wood that Marmaduke MacKurdy was delivering, but then I was reminded that these days, few mountain people could afford coal.

After returning from Illinois, I learned that a large conglomerate had bought most of the smaller mines and merged them into one large mining company named the Brocton Mining Company. The Brocton Company dug and shipped most of the mountain's coal off to buyers in the big cities. The conglomerate had the advantage of more capital and larger equipment. As a result, dozens and dozens of new miners were coming to the mountain. Wages were better for the miners flocking to the company's busy new enterprise. A new community called Brockton was established a few miles north of Harpsville where poor old John Mulley had been hanged. It was nearest the location of the thickest, if not the deepest, coal seams yet discovered on the mountain.

Instead of digging into the earth by way of small, stooping tunnels the new company was stripping away and removing the overburden of dozens of feet of earth to expose the coal beds. Now, enormous scars were appearing as open trenches dug through the ridges. This destruction was deeply resented by members of the original pioneer families on the mountain. A few small mines, like the one Mr. McDuffy worked, continued to deliver to local families and their operations earned enough extra income to keep their families from going hungry.

With the arrival of so many added hard-working miners coming to the mountain and the obvious need for some kind of entertainment or other distractions after a long day of hard labor, the moonshining industry began to boom. Families that had never before considered this undertaking were now turning to producing whiskey and were making a handsome profit. I never thought about the possibility of any of our family becoming involved until Otis said abruptly,

"Boogie, I'm not sure my family is going to make it. Dad's been sick most of the year so far. Most everything is gone; potatoes, flour, lard, and the hams in the meat house have been whittled down to practically bone. We've gotta keep our few chickens for the eggs and our cows for the little milk they provide for the babies. Mama cries a lot, and I can hear her late at night when she thinks the rest of us are sleeping. Uncle Harlan already has a new copper pot set up over in Oral Hollow. He has yeast and sugar hidden in the top of that shed out yonder. He says there is no shame in us making a little moonshine if it helps us feed our family. Grandma O'Mally agrees, saying there is no harm if one intends to drink in moderation, and she thinks every family has a right to have a still if for no other reason than to provide drink for medicinal purposes."

"I never liked the taste of moonshine whiskey myself. If, after taking a drink one finds it necessary to contort his face and shudder and then choke out "durn, that's good shine," then it surely ain't that good," I protested.

"You've never tasted whiskey, Boogie?" Otis asked.

"I never said I haven't tasted it. I said I never liked it."

I well remember back when I got my first taste of moonshine. I was about eight or ten years old. My friend, Larry Gully, and I were playing hide and seek in his family's backyard and I crawled under his family's home to hide. While there I found several quart fruit jars filled with some sort of clear liquid sitting on the tops of the floor joists. I could hear Larry outside, still leaning against a tree, calling out, "Eight, nine, ten, ready or not, here I come."

Curious as to those jars, I didn't wait to be found and I blurted out, "Hey Larry, I'm under here."

When he climbed under to join me, I asked him, "What is in all these jars?

"So, this is where they've been hiding it," he said. "This is my brother's hiding place for moonshine."

Larry's family's house sat on stone pillars and on top of those were heavy wooden floor joists which had provided a convenient space to hide dozens of quart fruit jars filled to the brim with white lightning. Lined along the tops of the beams were a dozen or so jars waiting for the brother's future customers. Our favorite discovery, however, was a fancy little flask with half its contents gone. It was evidently someone's private sipping whiskey that they had hidden until the next time their thirst got the better of them. Larry and I quickly removed it along with one of the full jars and headed down the hill to a small creek. Larry removed the cork from the flask and offered me a taste. Feeling all grown up, I turned the flask up and took a full swallow. Instead of the pleasant, good-tasting drink I had expected, it must have been filled with pure lava. I know my eyes bulged out of my head, and I surely breathed fire. Larry burst out laughing. He had known what was coming. I gagged and choked and felt fire passing out my nostrils. I think I could have punched him if I could have seen him through the tears that distorted my sight and filled my eyes. All I could see was several Larrys laughing and dancing around me.

"Come on, Boogie, don't be a wimp," he teased, "This is the way you drink it,"

He knelt and half-filled the pewter jar lid with creek water. then filled the rest of the lid with moonshine and diluted it slightly. He sloshed it around and then he took a long sip.

"Augh," he said while wiping his mouth with his shirt sleeve. "Now that was goooood!"

He poured another round, mixed it with creek water, and offered it to me.

"No," I said, still choking, "I don't need any more of that stuff."

"Try it diluted this way," he insisted it's not so bad when you mix it with water."

Cautiously, I lifted the lid to my lips. I managed to swallow a couple of gulps before I began choking again. I could still feel the fire in my throat and nostrils but admittedly it was not as bad as the first time.

Larry was still laughing at my discomfort when we noticed one of his brothers walk around the house and stoop to go under the floor. We realized that our theft from their cache would soon be discovered and thinking that he and his brothers would pound Larry and me to a bloody pulp, I at once abandoned my friend, splashed across that little creek, and half-ran, half-staggered toward home. I hurried as best as I could with my brow hot with sweat and the road spinning. I imagined his brother, or perhaps all of them, hurrying after me and ready to beat me silly for drinking their whiskey.

Arriving at my grandmother O'Mally's, I found the yard full of visiting cousins playing and having a wonderful time; Otis and Bobby Joe were there too, and being older, they realized I was just a bit tipsy.

"Quick, hide me," I begged.

"What's the matter, Boogie? You sick?"

"Yeah, I don't feel so good."

"Sit here," Otis said as he lowered me onto a bench. "I'll get your mother."

"No, no, I'm not that kind of sick. I think I am drunk, I think."

"Drunk. What in the world are you talking about?" Bobby Joe asked.

Fumbling in my pocket I pulled out the small flask from the Gully boy's stash. Without realizing it, I had fled without returning it to my friend Larry. Now I was sure I would be pursued by a horde of angry Gully brothers.

Otis, laughing at my predicament, took my arm, led me around my grandmother's house and ushered me into her musty-smelling fruit cellar. He prevented me from getting either a severe spanking from my mom or grandmother or possibly a beating from the Gully brothers. Unfortunately, with so many kids around they saw us and wanted to know if we were playing hide and seek. Otis told them no. Having been discovered in that hiding place, he decided to hide me under our great-grandmother's old house, which stood nearby. Her cellar would be safe since all the children thought our great-grandmother was a witch and her house and especially her cellar surely haunted. I suspected that she may have been a witch as well but was now too intoxicated to give a rat's butt. The coolness down in her cellar was soothing, and as I slumped onto the dirt floor, I slipped into a restful world of sleep.

My father and our Blackspaniel family shied away from moonshine, refusing to become involved in the whiskey trade. With my mom's family, the O'Mally's, it was a different story altogether.

Grandmother O'Mally felt that every family had the God-given right to own and operate a family still. I always thought her beliefs were slightly off-kilter since she was a good church-going Christian woman. I think she still resented any government official who dictated what a family could and could not do. I think it stemmed from the days of the Civil War after her grandfather, my great-grandfather, a private in the Confederate army, was captured over near Camac's Ferry and made to sign an oath to remain neutral until the end of the war. The federals shipped him off north of the Ohio River where he had to remain for almost two years until the war was over while working as a teamster. It seemed to my grandmother that after that, the government was always dictating what a southern family could and could not do and she resented it.

My mother's brothers, like the Tishams, ran a whiskey still discreetly hidden in one of the deeply secluded hollows on the mountain. The main difference between the O'Mallys and the Tishams was that the O'Mallys were fun to be around, easy to deal with, and seemed to love the company of their neighbors, except at their still. Uncle Rufus was everyone's favorite and probably mine as well. He was the youngest of six boys, slightly less than two years older than my mother, Dorothy. It was he and Cousin Otis who finally convinced me to come into the whiskey-making business with the O'Mally family.

I guess that was my initiation into a life of crime. As it turned out, I learned later the Gully boys never suspected me or their little brother for their missing whiskey. Each blamed the other and all were usually too inebriated to ever consider either Larry or me. Anyway, that incident somehow gained me an invitation to join Otis and his uncles for a brief period of moonshining. After Otis told our uncles of my goofy adventure they all enjoyed a good laugh and asked if I would consider helping them at their latest whiskey venture. First, they asked for my pledge to keep their enterprise a complete secret and I assured them it would be safe with me.

I had always suspected that my uncles had stills hidden somewhere on Grace Mountain and that Grandmother O'Mally may have even sanctioned it. Grandpa O'Mally had passed years ago and somehow the family seemed to prosper slightly more than others. I guess they never wanted us young'uns to know. A few times I questioned my grandmother O'Mally about my suspicions concerning different mountain families and she quickly defended their right to own a still.

"If it were used strictly for medicinal purposes," she would insist.

I was old enough to read between the lines. I also knew that when men saw their families hungry and ill-clothed, they would consider any line of work to provide food and comfort. The depression did that to folks. My daddy's family, especially Granddad and Grandma Blackspaniel, were dead set against whiskey. They followed saw-milling and advocated Christian ways. Any involvement I had in making whiskey would need to be kept confidential.

My excuse for an absence from my family for a couple of weeks was to be another of the annual camping and hunting trips with Otis, Bobby Joe, and me. It was something we enjoyed doing almost every fall and it would not draw any unnecessary attention to our real purpose, that of helping his uncles make a run of "mountain dew." My first introduction to the still and its location was under the ruse that Otis and I would hunt for deer, even though they were now a rare sight on the mountain. Squirrels and other small game were still plentiful. Bobby Joe was still with his uncle in Illinois so would miss this year's hunt. The following morning, Otis gathered his rifle and some extra shells, and we collected our sleeping gear, a few supplies, including a sack of Irish potatoes, a pail of lard, a jar of flour, some salt and pepper, a pot and pan and a couple of baked sweet potatoes each and headed out.

Otis and I followed a seldom-used path and were careful to conceal ourselves from any other folks we met along the way. At a point where a rocky wash intersected with our path we quickly entered into the forest and were careful to walk on the rocks to conceal our entry. Learning from Otis, I could see that he followed the ways of seasoned moonshiners in tactics that would keep our path to the still well-hidden. We followed the wash for a few hundred feet and then lightly stepped into a cushion of pine needles and weathered leaves. Otis always used a different approach each time to avoid leaving clues to our entry.

Deeper and deeper we continued into the dense thickets of the forest and through several hollows. Finally, we descended into the one known as Oral Hollow and into a heavier growth of mountain laurel and rhododendron. When we arrived at the bottom of the ravine, Otis indicated that this was our destination. I looked around expecting to find a flowing stream of water but instead, there was only a wet weather hollow.

"This doesn't seem to be a very suitable location for a moonshine still," I mumbled.

Otis turned and followed the dry wash upwards a couple of hundred feet more and to my astonishment we came to a steady stream of water bubbling up from under a rock ledge. It flowed over a few rocks and ledges and then immediately disappeared into a sinkhole.

"You see Boogie? This is a perfect location. Uncle Harlan found it while hunting coons. No revenuer will walk up a dry hollow looking for a working still." I agreed, "I don't think there could have been a better location to hide a moonshine operation on the mountain."

A few feet below the spring sat the recently constructed whiskey still, complete with a large copper pot, a copper tub, and seven or eight large wooden barrels of about fifty gallons each. Getting all this set up in this thicket must have taken weeks. The still was set under and against the rock bluff which was covered with a heavy growth of hemlock, laurel, and rhododendron. Uncles Rufus and Harlan had chosen this location well. The furnace and pot had been set up over the past couple of weeks and were now awaiting all the necessary ingredients. Otis's uncles had not arrived yet but were expected to be on their way, hauling in more supplies by mules: items like cornmeal for mash, bags of yeast, and sugar to help in fermentation. My job was to help Otis gather plenty of dry firewood of oak and hickory and be as discreet as possible. Otis even instructed me to help cover any of the evidence of our activity by collecting random dead brush or leaves to scatter over areas we had disturbed. This should help keep the still's location well hidden in case any passing hunter or nosy revenuer came by. We split the wood for the first fire as quietly as possible, even though the closest house I knew of was at least five miles distant. Once a fire was burning sufficiently inside the firebox, all one was required to do was to feed dry poles eight or ten feet long into the oven like feeding a pair of granddad's wet long johns into a hand-cranked clothes ringer. We quickly stored our wood, along with our axe and crosscut saw, under the overhanging rock ledge near the still.

Otis lightly tapped me on my shoulder, smiled, and said, "Good job, Boogie, now we just have to wait until Uncle Rufus arrives with our supplies."

We leaned back resting against the slope of the hillside. I was excited to be part of this new adventure. I lay there looking up, catching golden glimpses of sunlight dancing through the emerald canopy of leaves as a gentle breeze blew through the tall rhododendron. Birds seemed to be everywhere, chattering, and darting in and out of the brush. Their musical chirping was welcome. The sudden hush of the constant chattering would serve as a warning if an intruder approached but today they sang everywhere through the trees. The gurgling of the little stream as the water tumbled over the rocks and small ledges as it rushed down and disappeared into the sinkhole soothed any apprehension I had at taking part in any so-called illicit activity. We waited, enjoying those small voices of nature, with our heads resting on our pillowed hands. It was peaceful here below the ridge as we listened in the quiet for sounds of the uncles and the mules that we expected shortly from somewhere up the ridge.

"Otis, why does the government care if we make whiskey anyway if folks enjoy drinking it?"

"It's not that they care that people make it, and not so much that they drink it," Otis answered. "It's the fact that the government isn't receiving any taxes from the whiskey made and sold here in the mountains. The government wants a share in taxes on everything."

"What happens if we are discovered?" I asked Otis.

"What cha mean Boogie?" Otis questioned.

"What happens if we are found and there is gunplay? Remember the Tisham boys?"

"Well, Uncle Rufus says if for some reason we were caught, just give up. He doesn't believe in gun fights. Besides most all the deputies are our friends and hurting a friend just isn't worth it."

I liked hearing those reassuring words. I surely didn't want to hurt anyone or be hurt, especially by any friend.

We lay there thinking and waiting. Finally, we heard someone talking in muted tones up the ridge. Staying quiet and listening as they grew closer. Otis told me to move to the top of the rocky ledge behind us, hide, and wait. He moved off through the brush in the direction of the approaching sounds. It was quiet for a few minutes and then I could hear men happily greeting each other. Their voices grew more recognizable as they approached our still site.

"Boogie, come on down. It's Uncles Rufus and Harlan."

I eased from my hiding place, came down from the bluff, and helped them unload the burden from the two mules. I guessed there must have been about ten bushels of corn. Everything was stored safely inside the empty wooden barrels until tomorrow. Once the lids were secured to prevent any raccoon or other varmints from damaging our supplies, we led the mules away by a different route. Once we were out of the woods, we mounted the two mules with Otis behind his Uncle Rufus and me behind Uncle Harlan. We would sleep at Rufus's cabin tonight and come back early tomorrow morning to resume our "camping trip."

The next morning, we all left before daylight to avoid any prying eyes. We each carried heavy sacks of sugar and smaller ones filled with rye. On later trips, we each carried in tow sacks filled with washed and dried fruit jars and lids. Uncles Rufus and Harlan had packed everything carefully to prevent breaking or clinking loudly as we walked through the woods. I was pretty tired by the time we reached our still site; I think we all were. The weather was cool but the walk through the woods while carrying our burdens of glass still tired everyone out. We wiped our brows with our handkerchiefs, and everyone sat resting for a couple of minutes before Harlan rose and moved to the stack of wood Otis and I had stored. He took pieces of kindling and started a fire inside a small nook against the rock bluff, then moved the copper tub to a spot near the fire and began to fill it with water.

"What is he doing?" I asked. "I thought the fire should be built in the firebox."

"He is getting ready to make mash for the beer," Otis said. "The furnace won't be needed for another week or so. It's a long, drawn-out process, Boogie. Remember when the Tishams held me and Bobby Joe until their run was finished?"

Harlan instructed Otis and me to finish filling the tub with water while he got the fire blazing to gradually heat its contents. Once the water had warmed sufficiently, he added nearly a bushel and a half of beautiful, full-kernel, white corn.

"Now, we'll give it a couple of days," he said, smiling.

Rufus and Harlan moved to the sacks of corn and corn meal they had brought in with the mules and cut them open with a hunting knife. They were already well-sprouted.

"Your pappy helped us with fermenting this corn," Harlan said laughing.

"No way," I countered.

"Oh, he didn't know it. We just covered our sacks of corn in the back of his sawdust pile after he had left work for the day. We allowed the heat generated by rotting sawdust do our job. Of course, we had to do a little digging to find it after his crew had added a couple of days of fresh sawdust from all the logs they sawed."

Rufus removed a large sausage grinder from a bag and handed it to Otis and told us to grind the remaining corn into a five-gallon bucket.

"Boy," I said, "The process of making moonshine is a bit more complicated than I had imagined."

"Boogie, we are just getting started." Otis joked.

Once the tub was sufficiently warmed throughout, we stirred it up well, covered it, and allowed it to sit for at least twenty-four hours. After a full day, we drained off the water and moved the contents to a sprouting tub. Once again, we filled the tub with warm water but this time drained it off after about fifteen minutes and then moved the tub toward the fire to apply a good steady heat. Mine and Otis's job at this point was to occasionally turn the cooler side of the tub toward the heat and keep its contents evenly warm. It was necessary to repeat these steps every day for about five days and to occasionally mix the contents on the bottom upward. Soon we had malt which was all producing good sprouts.

"Now, we can build the fire in the furnace, Boogie," Otis announced.

I gathered plenty of kindling and then heavier firewood and we soon had a fire burning within the furnace which rose up and heated the copper pot. Rufus and Harlan had placed a hollow log from the spring to the opening in the cap of the still to transfer the cool, mountain water to begin filling the large container. After the pot was full and the water had warmed sufficiently, Harlan slowly poured in a half bushel of corn meal while Rufus stirred it in well. Now, we stood anxiously waiting as it came to a slow boil. As it bubbled, Rufus continued to stir it slowly for at least another forty minutes.

"Okay, boys," Harlan said. "Roll over one of those wooden barrels."

Otis and I rolled one over and placed it under what Otis called the slop arm. Harlan pushed in a "plug stick" and the hot contents of the still began to fill the barrel.

"Here Boogie," Harlan said while handing me a sack of uncooked cornmeal. "Pour just a gallon of this into the barrel and be sure to stir it in good. The heat in the barrel will cook it sufficiently."

I followed his directions.

"Okay, that's good for that barrel. Now move it aside and bring me another one" Harlan instructed.

We repeated the process each time until all the wooden barrels were filled and lined up, side by side, under the edge of the rock ledge.

"Now we can go home, clean up and rest, boys. We can all use a good bath cause we stink worse than Billy Goats." Rufus said laughing.

Arriving back at Rufus's home, we gathered a bar of soap and fresh linen and headed down to a small creek where a pool of water would be suitable for bathing. We stripped down to our birthday suits, and each splashed awkwardly into the chilly water. And boy, was it cold. We all shrieked loudly, quickly submerged, and, while shivering, washed vigorously while trying our best to lather up. We laughed while playfully splashing each other, and then we did our best to cleanse our bodies from the filth of the day's labor at the still. While the rest of us were in a hurry to bathe, Rufus had thoughtfully lingered long enough to build a warming fire and after toweling off, we stood huddled around it in our underwear enjoying the heat, telling jokes, and sharing wild stories.

After a good supper of beans, taters, and turnip greens, we turned in. It was hardly dark yet outside, but we were tired. Brothers Rufus and Harlan shared the only bed which sat off to one side of the small room that served as the cabin's living room and bedroom. Otis and I bedded down on pallets laid out near the fireplace. The uncles were snoring loudly before either Otis or I could fall asleep.

"Boogie, anyone ever told you the story of the time ole Tater Carson left the mountain?"

"I remember hearing of him, but he was on the mountain before my time, or at least back when I was just a small child."

"It was back in 1919 or 1920, as best as I can remember," Otis continued. "Tater came to the mountain from somewhere down near Broomtown Valley. He was known as a kind of a misfit. Always in some kind of trouble. Anyway, our great Uncle Walter hired him to help with his whiskey still way back up in Fryer Hollow over near the bluffs. Tater's main job was to hide the new jars and jugs of whiskey in a certain spot after it was run off. After each run, he would pack it into an old bag and disappear into the thicket headed to the hiding place. In forty-five minutes or so, he would return for his next load. Old Tater seemed to be doing a good job and Walter was well satisfied with him. That is until the day Uncle went by the hiding place to check his inventory before the buyer came for delivery. Counting and re-counting, he found his cache short by a dozen quarts."

"That was a sizable shortage," I said.

"Suspecting Tater was responsible, Uncle Walter brought his best coon hound to the still site. In a bag, he had put in an old coon skin. While Tater was busy collecting the full jars, Uncle Walter took that old coon skin and rubbed its scent all over Tater's carrying bag. Tater returned with the last of the whiskey, filled his bag, and off through the brush he went. Uncle Walter allowed him all the time he needed before siccing his old hound on Tater's trail. Straining at his leash, that old hound pulled Walter through the thicket, hot on Tater's trail. It was at least a quarter of a mile before Uncle came to a tall beech tree with a large cavity at its base. Inside was a bulge of dead leaves and brush which when removed, revealed all of Walter's missing whiskey.

Tater Carson had no clue his jig was up. After adding a part of the day's jars to the collection in the beech tree, he continued to Uncle Walter's hiding place. Now Walter was in hot pursuit, and his anger was festering. Then he decided to wait and not confront Tater just yet. He quietly returned to the location of his still. He had a plan and informed his other two youthful partners of his intentions. Soon Tater returned with his empty bag.

"Any problems?" Uncle Walter asked.

"Nope, everything went as usual," Tater replied.

Everyone remained quiet and they began dismantling the still.

"What, are we done?" Tater questioned.

"Yep, we're done. Finished the run and it's time to move on," said Uncle Walter.

"Can I collect my wages now? I guess I'll be headed home."

"How much you think I'll be owing you now Tater?" Uncle Walter asked.

"Well, you promised me fifty cents a day and we've been out here nine or ten days now, so I figure about five dollars."

"Five dollars it is, then. I want to keep my part of the bargain," Uncle said.

"Tater's eyes brightened when Uncle Thomas placed five silver dollars in coin in the palm of Tater's filthy hand.

"Now, what do you plan to do with my whiskey you have hidden in that big beech up the ridge?"

Tater's smile flattened, and his expression took on a frown of disbelief, then panic.

"I never, I never," he stuttered as he began to back away.

Walter's helpers were standing just behind Tater, and as he turned to flee, he found his path blocked and escape impossible. Tater begged for mercy, but they bound his hands to the trunk of a twisted sourwood and stripped his shirt from his back.

"Please," he begged. "I'll never steal from you again."

It was too late; he already had. Walter cut a length of hickory and began to whip poor Tater without mercy, at least twenty good, cutting-the-flesh lashes. Tater twisted, kicked, begged, and cried as Uncle Walter laid it on, but Walter intended to teach him a lesson he would never forget. As he finished, Tater hung there writhing and whimpering in pain.

"Tater," he said, "I want you to leave this mountain, and if we ever catch you up here in the future, your family will never see you again. Do you understand?"

"Yes, I understand."

The boys untied Tater, and he turned to Uncle Walter and spoke, "I am sorry." He handed him the five silver coins.

"No, Tater'" uncle said. "We had an agreement, and I have kept my part of it. You'll probably be needing most of it anyway, for salve for those whelps on your backside."

"Ole Tater limped away through the brush and was never seen on the mountain again."

I lay there on the pallet, thinking of the story Otis had just told. Uncles Rufus and Harlan were still snoring. Otis grew quiet, and I continued to think of the story of poor Tater. Then I dozed off as well.

The morning came earlier than I wanted, but we had plenty of work left to do. We packed the last of the supplies into our carrying sacks and headed off into the wee hours of early morning. The last hooting of an owl echoed clearly from the direction of Oral Hollow.

"Our nightwatchman is sounding; all clear," Harlan said with a grin of approval.

We walked within a few hundred yards of our still, and we discovered the ground had been literally plowed during the night, apparently by feral hogs searching for acorns.

"Well, this is not a good sign," Rufus said. "If they catch wind of our mash, they could ruin our operation."

Wild pigs love corn mash, and if they found our still, they could cause severe damage or even destroy it entirely while rooting to get to the mash. We hurried toward our workplace. Happily, there was no evidence that the herd had found it yet, but both uncles agreed it would only be a matter of time. We all busied ourselves constructing a strong, secure log enclosure around the perimeter of our equipment. We gathered an abundance of scattered rocks and heavily reinforced the inside of our log embankment. It would be next to impossible for the hogs to do any damage.

"Now It's time to finish making our whiskey," Harlan said as he stood and reached for the stirring stick. "We need to see just how thick our mixture is."

He placed the stick upright in the center of the barrel, and it stood there without tilting it to either side.

"It's a still bit thick," he announced. Pour in a little water slowly while I stir."

I poured while he stirred until, finally, the stick fell easily to the edge of the barrel. We repeated the process with each barrel until all the mash was thinned evenly. At this point, Rufus added a gallon of malt to each barrel, stirred it in well, and then added a double handful of rye which he sprinkled evenly over the tops of the barrels. Then we waited until it formed a cap that would eventually hold a bead. Finally, we added ten pounds of sugar to each barrel, covered the barrels and allowed the ingredients to work until we had a fine beer. While we waited, Rufus and Harlan went home to deal with personal business and Otis and I continued to "camp and hunt." Our job now while waiting was to watch the mixture and to occasionally stir it well to ensure it continued to form properly.

At this juncture, Otis and I had time to do some hunting and we chose as our quarry one of the fat hogs that continued to feast under the large white oak trees in search of the abundant acorns and chestnuts that covered the ground. As they rooted each night, they came closer and closer to our still and we didn't want them smelling our mash. We decided a nice hog would be a welcome item for our family's tables as fall changed to winter. From our camp, we followed the crest of the ridge south for about a quarter of a mile and found a well-used animal trail that crossed the ridge and descended into a thick cover of rhododendrons and across a rapidly flowing mountain stream. We chose as our blind an open space where we could watch the trail on our side of the creek and also the upper part of the trail coming down the ridge on the opposite side of the stream. The laurel and rhododendrons obscured part of our view along the creek banks.

The scene was unspoiled, pastoral, and an utterly fine example of a wilderness. We backed into a clustered growth of young hemlocks and their soft green branches embraced us. All around us were holly trees, towering hemlocks, and tall, slender poplars. A thin morning mist dampened and quietened the sounds of any grass and the leaves where we waited. A woodpecker on a dead limb high above us was busy drilling for its morning meal, its chiseled shavings showering us with debris. As I looked up, my attention was attracted to a tall, slender sapling where I noticed a young raccoon playfully watching us as if playing hide and seek. We stood silent, watching and enjoying the wonders of nature while waiting for our quarry to appear.

Soon our attention was attracted to a twig snapping on the side of the far ridge. We couldn't yet see what had broken the limb but could hear the heavy rustling of leaves. A hunter, I thought. No animal would be making that much noise. Disappointed that another human would come so far into the wilderness with so much disregard for the serenity of nature disappointed me. Otis and I remained hidden in our blind and Otis relaxed his grip on his rifle. Agitated, we waited for the hunter to approach. Then, to our total disbelief there appeared on the trail opposite us a large, black bear lumbering down the game trail straight toward us.

"No way," I whispered nervously as I grabbed Otis's arm.

All Otis said was, "Oh, crap!"

There hadn't been a bear reported on Grace Mountain in over forty years. The last known bear was killed by a group of hunters led by our great-grandpa down on Bear Creek, and that was way before either Otis or I was born. We were stunned and in denial, yet this large bear was sauntering toward us.

"What are we going to do?" I questioned.

"Well, I'm certainly not going to shoot a bear with this flimsy old gun," Otis said firmly. "You remember all the stories told of how an injured bear often mauls and kills the hunter?"

"But it's headed straight for us," I said becoming more agitated.

"Here Boogie," he said, trying to hand the rifle to me. "You want him shot; you shoot him. I'm going to climb this tree."

"No, don't climb any tree. Bears can outclimb either one of us, and you know it."

I neither took the gun nor said another word but was terrified as the bear continued toward us. I hoped that he would stop at the mountain stream that separated us from each other. I prayed that he would not see us or catch our scent. Closer and closer he came until he finally reached the edge of the creek. Instead of crossing, he waded into the shallow creek and began turning over the flat stones apparently searching for tasty crawdads. He was busy splashing about while pursuing his quarry and making lots of noise as he followed the stream away from Otis and me. Finally, he disappeared from our view behind the dense growth of mountain laurel and rhododendrons along the stream bank. We could still hear him turning over rocks and splashing after frogs, fish, or crawdads. Then, finally, all grew silent, and I breathed a long sigh of relief. We waited quietly, still hidden in the thickness of those small hemlocks. We both wanted to be sure the bear had continued on. It was then that all hell broke loose.

Suddenly, there was a wild crash in the direction the bear had gone. I heard a tremendous uproar of crashing and squealing, and it sounded like all the brush in the forest was being plowed through like a small tornado roaring toward us. Hearing the ruckus, my mind raced for answers. Had the bear caught our scent and was charging toward us in a mad, wild panic? Suddenly, there were a dozen or more dark shapes rushing toward us, crashing through the brush. Now we both panicked, and Otis readied his gun. I thought there were far more assailants than we had bullets. Then, to our surprise, we saw that we were being overrun by a herd of wild pigs. Big ones, little ones, and some that looked like chipmunks because of their stripes were running on all sides of us. The bear, as he followed the stream had stumbled on a large herd of hogs that had bedded down near the creek in the laurel thickets. The adult hogs were accompanied by more than a dozen small piglets that were now fleeing past us and squealing frantically. Wild hogs in the mountains had a reputation for being notoriously dangerous.

"Shoot, shoot!" I urged Otis.

He brought his gun up and fired at one of the sows running past us. I should warn you that witnessing an animal being killed is not a pleasant spectacle. At the instant of the blast, the missile exploded a shower of blood from the hog's shoulder. The hog, its adrenaline pumping, continued its desperate flight. With every pulse of its heart, a spurt of vermilion squirted into the air and the hog continued to squeal frantically. Fortunately, death came quickly. After running a few yards more, the hog fell, plowing into the earth and then she lay quietly. I could see the last spasms of her legs kicking as she tried to flee even in the last throes of death.

The sounds of the other members of the herd were fading now as they fled across the ridge. A single piglet, cute and striped like a chipmunk, ran in circles around us, separated from the others. Then it became eerily quiet again. Otis and I, both still nervous, remained stationary, listening for any sounds of the bear that might still be prowling nearby. The young raccoon I had noticed earlier was now clinging precariously to the uppermost branches of a tall poplar and in his fright could climb no higher.

I was slightly traumatized by the tragic events leading to the shooting of that poor hog but at the same time elated that now our ruse of hunting had gained some legitimacy. Our families would be proud of the extra meat Otis and I added to our tables. We quickly moved to the kill and began the process of field dressing and readying it for transport home. After the hog was dressed, we found the task of hanging it high up and out of the reach of a hungry bear extremely difficult. We guessed that, after dressing, the hog would weigh at least 120 to 130 pounds. We threw a stout length of hemp rope across a limb, tied one end securely around the hog's ankles and the other end to a good-sized sapling which, when pulled down, helped to winch the hog's weight up. With Otis lifting the hog and me pulling down on that sapling we leveraged the hog up and out of the reach of the bear and to where it would be safe hanging in the cool mountain air.

Later that evening when Uncle Rufus came by the still to check our progress, we excitedly told him our story of seeing a bear.

"Boys," he said, "have y'all been nipping at the beer? There hasn't been a bear seen on Grace Mountain in over forty years."

With both Otis and me insisting that we had really seen a bear and a large one, Rufus finally admitted that it was possible that one could have wandered over from the higher mountains that loomed up to the east of us. He asked us to keep it our secret because any reports of a bear on the mountain would cause a rush of hunters to descend into Oral Hollow and that could lead to the discovery of our still. Frustrated at not being able to share our story gripped us but we agreed it would be bad for our still and worse for the poor bear. I was proud that at least one bear remained somewhere on Grace Mountain.

Then we turned our attention to the hog. We were proud of our hunting success and eager to show Rufus our trophy. Otis and I then eagerly led him to the site where the hog hung and explained the circumstances of our hunting success. Rufus agreed to bring in the mules on the following morning and haul out our heavy load of pork butt, hams and shoulders. Our families would be proud of us when the delicious aroma of barbecue permeated from the air from our firepits and grill.

The sealed brew in our still was allowed to ferment for two to three weeks. When the time came, we busied ourselves with removing the caps and I at once smelled the strong odor of alcohol. A layer of foam covered the surface. The alcohol had eaten most of the layer off the top and now our beer was ready to distill. Otis and I strained the liquid through several cheese-cloths to remove the rest of the crust and sealed all the connections to the still with a thick rye paste. Next, we poured the strained contents into the still and Harlan kindled a fire inside the furnace underneath. We stirred slowly while allowing our beer to heat evenly until our thermometer reached a temperature of 150°F. Harlan stoked our fire and pushed in lengths of fresh logs. While continuing to slowly stir, we brought the temperature up to and kept it at 190°F. Now, the cap of the still and the cap arm were connected and sealed, and we were cooking off our run. Finally, after weeks of preparation, we were in the final stages of making our whiskey.

"Whoopee!" Otis called out.

Harlan laughed and cautioned us to not get too elated. We still had work ahead of us. I started wondering how I would explain any extra money from the sale of our whiskey to my mom and Pa Blackspaniel.

We adjusted our pipes and allowed our condenser to fill with cold water from the spring. Rufus instructed us to always fill it from the bottom and allow it to empty from the top. That would ensure that the cool water was constantly circulating upward and around our condensing coil. After a few minutes, the first drop of our labor dripped from the end of our worm.

Now everyone was smiling. Harlan stuck his finger under the drip and placed it on his tongue.

He smiled and said, "Boys, I think we have a winner."

We all congratulated each other and got our jars and jugs ready to fill with some of the best "mountain dew" on Grace Mountain.

Harlan placed a large funnel under the end of the worm and filled it with well-washed charcoal.

"That will filter out some of the crud," he said.

As the jugs and jars were filled and sealed, Rufus handed us each a carrying bag. We wrapped our containers carefully, filled our bags, and carried them to the hiding place up a side hollow and near an abandoned sawmill road. Rufus said it would be close to the road where the bootlegger could easily pick it up. Our burden was heavy and each of us was pretty much exhausted when we arrived at the secret spot. As we approached, I was puzzled to see a large, aged beech with a cavity partway up its trunk.

"No way," I said. "Surely this is not the same tree used by Tater years ago."

"It sure is." Rufus said, smiling, "Me and your uncle Harlan were the two kids working with your great-uncle Walter back then."

Then I noticed the carvings in the aged bark of that old beech. There was the whittled outline of a human hand holding a crucifix and the initials R. O. and H. O. with the date 1919. Understandably, Tater had failed to carve his initials there.

Over the next couple of days, we continued to fill our jars and jugs with homebrew and carry them to be hidden in that massive beech tree. Finally, the day came for the bootlegger to come pick it all up and Hiram had us start moving it to a convenient loading area near the road. This part of the whiskey business is critical. All your hard work is now sitting near the road waiting to be loaded before someone comes along to discover your clandestine activities. Otis waited patiently while I paced back and forth. Finally, off in the distance, we heard the sounds of an approaching vehicle. At first, the sound was wavering as the vehicle dropped into a hollow and then grew louder again when it gained the summit of a rise, still chugging along steadily in our direction. The sound of the engine was vaguely familiar and I wondered where I had heard it before. Then it stopped and a horn tooted to alert us to its arrival. We gathered our stash of whiskey and walked briskly to the waiting truck. I was shocked to see that the driver was none other than Marmaduke MacKurdy himself. He didn't recognize me and I pulled the brim of my worn hat down more snuggly over my hidden face. Marmaduke promptly lifted a panel on either side of his truck bed to reveal the hidden compartments where he hid and hauled his contraband whiskey. As the jars were carefully inserted into each cubby hole, handfuls of sawdust were packed around each to protect it from the constant jarring as the truck bounced over the country roads.

    Who would have suspected poor old, crippled Marmaduke? He had devised a perfect setup. Under the guise of delivering firewood to needy hillbilly families, he had the freedom to drive anywhere on the mountain without causing the least suspicion. Most all the mountain folk appreciated Marmaduke for his clever work. He openly delivered his firewood to the remotest families while secretly delivering moonshine to his waiting customers without raising the slightest suspicions of the authorities. I suspected some of those were among his best customers anyway.

Marmaduke was wiser than most. He rarely if ever tasted whiskey himself. Staying sober was the best way to remain in the mainstream and obscure. He understood that his loyal customers remained loyal for a reason and he trusted that Rufus and Harlan made the best whiskey available. None of his customers ever disagreed. The authorities who had occasion to approach him closely and speak with him always found him sober and agreeable and had no reason to suspect he was a thriving bootlegger. He did, however, seem to always have a chaw of tobacco tucked between his cheek and gum, and he could perpetually be heard humming a little ditty, something about rowing across a river called the Wide Tomorrow.

Marmaduke and his wife operated a small grocery store from their old board and log home out on Big Grove Mountain not too many miles from my grandparents. Their home had stood since the earliest years built by a family that later packed their belongings into a covered wagon and left the mountain for the wilds of Texas. I stopped at Marmaduke's store a couple of times when working at the sawmill in Easy Gap to buy soda pops and the makings of a bologna sandwich. I never suspected that he moonlighted as a bootlegger.

Chapter Twenty-four
Bitter Betrayal

Sam Pinkney fared better than I did at romance. He and the young lady he courted in Angel's Switch continued in love and eventually were married. Pinkney quit the sawmill and chose to settle down in the Switch. He and I had been best friends for several years while working at the various sawmills. Now it had been a couple of years since I last saw him, and I missed my friend. I understand he now owns a small construction company. God knows he has handled plenty of boards in his time and surely knows how to saw and nail them into the shape of a home. I often think of him and wonder how he is doing. I guess I may be a bit envious thinking of how lucky he was to marry the girl of his dreams when I did not. Still, I can't help but think of Willow and her husband Francois and I always pray he treats her well and that they are happy.

One day when I got home my mom handed me a letter. The return address was "Sam Pinkney, Angel's Switch, Tennessee." It was from Sam, and he shared all the latest news concerning his family and how his construction business had slowed, but somehow, he still managed to pay the bills. He invited me to stop for a visit the next time I traveled through the switch. A few weeks later, I happened to have business over in Centerville, and I made it a point to stop and visit my friend as I passed near his home on my return. He was all smiles and happy with his new life. I was surprised to find that he had a new addition to his family, a beautiful little daughter. Sam Pinkney had done well for himself. However, he shared other news that shook me to the core. Willow had recently been widowed when her husband Francois suddenly committed suicide. It seemed his employers at the Great Southern Railroad discovered a theft of funds and several other discrepancies with the records. The threat of prison time was more than the pompous mama's boy could bear. Pinkney heard that he put a gun to his head and blew his egotistical brains out.

More astonishing to me was the fact, that as they were going through his effects, a bundle of letters was found hidden in the back of one of his desk drawers. They were addressed to Miss Willow Countess, Angel's Switch, Tennessee, from Daniel Blackspaniel, Five Corners, Georgia.

"Oh God.' I shuddered. "Poor Willow; she must be going through hell."

"I'm afraid she isn't doing well at all," Pinkney said.

"Where is she? I should go see her." I said.

"She lives back with her mother, up in that white house. Her father passed not too long after Francois killed himself. Mr. Countess died suddenly from a heart attack while sitting in his church pew. The parson was ranting and condemning poor Willow for the tragic death of his son. Mr. Countess became noticeably upset and when he tried to rise, uttered a hoarse groan and fell flat on his face, dead! I understand poor Willow doesn't seem to want to live anymore."

"Surely, there is something I can do. I should try to see her if her mother would allow it."

As much as I am ashamed to admit it, I was both distraught and elated at the same time. I was deeply saddened for poor Willow, but I was also encouraged that I might give her hope in her time of need. I still loved her! I had loved Willow from the day I first met her and would honestly love her for the rest of my days.

"Daniel, there is more," Pinkney continued. "She has a son now, just a year older than my little girl. He is a cute little fellow, full of energy and very loving. I am afraid he is more than Willow can handle considering her condition and her mother seems to resent the child because of the sins of his father."

"I'll go visit Willow and see if I can be of any help."

I loaded back in Father's truck and proceeded up the mountainside to the Countess' residence. I parked in front of what had been a white picket fence but now found the paint tattered and curled. I drew a deep breath and sought the courage to approach the door. After knocking, I nervously stepped back a few steps and waited. After a time, the door opened slightly and Mrs. Countess peered through the narrow crack. She stood there for a moment without saying a word but finally managed to acknowledge me.

"Hello Daniel," she said faintly, "Won't you come in?"

I was surprised when she invited me inside her home, but I guess her arrogant, holier-than-thou attitude had been dismantled and she had lost hope of finding a husband of her choice for her daughter.

She escorted me to the parlor and invited me to sit in a cushioned chair that I assumed must have been Mr. Countess's favorite. She left the room, and after several minutes, I sensed the presence of someone standing in a doorway to my right. Looking up I was disheartened to see Willow dressed in her nightgown and robe. Her eyes were hollow, her hair unkempt and her features haggard. She was almost unrecognizable. I immediately stood and waited. She walked feebly to another chair and sank slowly onto its edge.

"Hello Daniel," she barely managed.

"Hello, Willow; it's good to see you," I said, trying to appear strong.

Inside I was terrified. What had happened to the beautiful girl I had known?

"Daniel I am so, so sorry. I screwed up big time. I am so sorry," she repeated.

Desperate, I asked, "Willow, what can I do? I want to help if I can."

I watched as tears streamed down her face; she sat limp while wringing her hands. I walked to her, sank to my knees, and took her hands in mine.

"Willow," I pleaded, "We can work this out. It's not too late."

Still crying she leaned forward and pressed her face against my chest. She said nothing, and together, we rocked slightly back and forth.

"I love you, Willow. I have loved you from the first day I saw you behind that postal counter. I'll always love you, then, now, and forever."

With my confession, she burst into tears. She cried so hard she trembled. From a partly opened doorway, I could see her mother standing and sobbing with remorse. I think, finally, her arrogance was replaced with an understanding heart. I think she had accepted me.

My embrace with Willow could have lasted for an eternity, but I knew she was exhausted. I wanted her to rest. I rose and told her I needed to return my father's truck but that I would return as soon as possible.

"Please be strong for me," I begged.

"Maybe I can be better prepared when you return." she said.

She tried to rise but I said, "I will let myself out. You rest. I'll see you within a few days."

I returned to my friend Sam Pinkney's and thanked him for his help. He kindly invited me to stay the night at his home, but I explained that I would need to return Father's truck and asked that he check on Willow until I could return. I explained that we still had a difficult situation with the Tishams to deal with.

Chapter Twenty-five
Tabors Mercantile

My Uncle Tabor O'Mally's store became a favorite hangout for many of the folks living on Grace Mountain. Men could buy petroleum products for their automobiles and women could buy the basic food and household items, like bread, milk, and cheese. Kids could find colas, candy, and chewing gum, and then enjoy swimming at Uncle Morris's pond across the road. Uncle Tabor realized he needed more storage and found it necessary to build an addition to his store to house his growing inventory. My cousin Otis was assisting him with the construction and my little brother June Bug was also there most of the time, eagerly picking up scattered materials and straightening bent nails for re-use. Uncle Tabor appreciated his help and paid him twenty-five cents an hour. June Bug walked around with all the swagger of a fully employed laborer.

On this day, Uncle Tabor was on the roof applying tin to his addition, and Otis shouldered another load to carry up the ladder. June Bug ran eagerly to hold the ladder steady as Otis stepped up on the bottom rung. A single shot from a shotgun rang out and Otis gave a painful yell. His load of tin slipped from his shoulder and dropped heavily on June Bug, knocking him to the ground. Otis rolled about, clutching his stomach, and blood began seeping through his overalls. He hoarsely yelled obscenities toward an unknown assailant. Hearing the simultaneous blast of a gun and Otis's painful cry, Uncle Tabor quickly rose and, as he mounted the top of the ladder, called out, "Otis, are you shot? Are you hit?"

Otis was rolling back and forth. You could hear the air wheezing through the ragged, bloodstained hole in his abdomen.

"I'm hurt, and I can't breathe, but you need to help June Bug. Get that roofing off him before he suffocates."

Uncle Tabor quickly descended the ladder while muttering something about catching a glimpse of none other than Doyle and Doolittle Tisham dashing off through the brush. He stooped to remove the loose tin from June Bug and then saw the blood oozing from his ear. June Bug lay motionless.

"June Bug, June Bug!" he pleaded with desperation. "Otis, Jesse's been shot, and he is not responding! I don't think he is breathing."

Otis moaned painfully and rolled toward June Bug. He pulled June Bug toward him and lay with his head across his lap.

June Bug never responded and lay limp in Otis's lap, "Oh, Uncle, I'm afraid June Bug is dead."

He managed a weak "June Bug, I am sorry."

Uncle Tabor walked without purpose, pacing back and forth asking God to please take care of his nephew Jesse and to heal his nephew Otis.

It was an hour later when Uncle Tabor arrived at the sawmill where my father worked. He had driven to the site as quickly as possible and slid to a halt. Father knew that something terrible must have happened and quickly shut off the mill. He approached Uncle Tabor, afraid to ask why he was there.

"Shy," he gasped, "Jesse was shot today, and I am afraid he didn't make it."

"What? What do you mean, Jesse's been killed?"

"It was those Tisham boys. I saw them running away through the brush. They were shooting at Otis and June Bug was just in the way."

My father slumped and leaned against his wagon. Tears were streaming down his dust-covered face. He drew shallow breaths and sat aimlessly; his thoughts lost and searching.

Then he asked, "Will Otis make it?"

"Yeah, Otis is hurt, but I think he will be okay. They've sent for the doctor down in Trickum."

My father continued sitting, slumped against the wagon wheel, staring into the unknown. Finally, wiping the tears from his face he staggered to his feet and thanked Uncle Tabor for coming to the mill first.

"I need to tell Dorothy. I don't know if she can handle such sad news. Poor June Bug, we will surely miss him."

I pulled my father's truck into his driveway and was surprised to find several buggies, wagons, and automobiles parked haphazardly across the yard. I could see my father and several other folks on the porch, all standing with downcast postures. As I was opening the truck door, he was already walking toward me and I was surprised, as this was unusual. I noticed he wore an expression of pain, and his eyes were red from tears. With his voice trembling, he spoke.

"Daniel," he said, "I have some bad news."

I waited, leaning against the open truck door.

"What, Dad, is it, Mom? "What's happened?"

"No son, it's June Bug; he has been killed."

"What?" I asked in disbelief. I sat there stunned and confused while trying to process what he had said. Knots were tightening in my stomach.

"It was the Tisham boys. They were apparently after your cousin, Otis. Otis was severely wounded but June Bug was killed."

This news made me feel like a mule had kicked me in the stomach. I crumpled to my knees. "Oh, Daddy. What will we do?" I cried.

We must comfort your mother. She is in shock and considerably fragile right now. I am worried about her.

I rose and walked toward the house. Entering our home, I found Mother seated at the kitchen table with several family members and friends gathered around. A few, feeling compelled to offer condolences, approached and embraced me, but I wasn't ready for hugs. I was not prepared for the sad realities that awaited me. June Bug was lying on a daybed on one side of the room. He appeared to be resting except for an unexpected pasty appearance. Our grandparents, aunts, and uncles sobbed in the shadows. Low mumbles were exchanged by neighbors, but I never heard them as my thoughts were lost in the great suffering of my heart. My best friend, my little brother, was shot for no reason of his own. Killed in a senseless act of revenge by ruthless brothers who had no regard for life or decency. Now, the anger swelled inside me, and I swore I would find the Tishams myself and even the score.

I heard the angry oaths sworn by my uncles. Until now the lawless acts of the Tishams had been tolerated by the O'Mally clan. Although they had committed heinous crimes against the county and its deputies they had never trespassed on the O'Mallys. Now, the old law of an eye for an eye became our oath, and the clan demanded retribution. The O'Mallys were soon arming themselves and were determined to find the Tishams and bring them to justice. Sheriff John Graham Hiram welcomed the addition of our clan into his group of deputies, but he cautioned against rushing headlong into a confrontation with the killers. He demanded discipline, and once everyone agreed, he swore them in as deputies and they were ready for combat.

The O'Mallys' knowledge of all the best places to hide on Grace Mountain was superior to that of the Tishams. The O'Mallys had lived on the mountain since arriving here in the late 1830s. They were descended from the original Scots-Irish immigrants who came to the mountain, traded, and later married the Indians and were some of the ancestors of the mysterious Melungeon race. The Tishams arrived on the mountain a full century later when ole Wash fled from their haunt on Flounder's Island. Sheriff Hiram recognized that with the cooperation of the O'Mally clan, he now had the best intelligence available. He divided his posse into four well-armed groups; each was led by one of the O'Mally brothers. He intended to discover the outlaws, completely surround them, and approach from all four sides to prevent any possible escape. Now, his deputies scoured the mountain with instructions to find the outlaws, but not to confront them when they discovered. Instead, he wanted to wait until he could bring his full posse together to make the capture successful.

Unfortunately, the Tishams were no longer acting alone, nor had they been weakened by years of confrontation with the law. On the contrary, they were strengthened by the addition of clan members and rogue neighbors who viewed them as champions of the disadvantaged. Together, they rejected any laws or rules contrary to their traditional way of life. They were a ruthless gang of marauding bootleggers and their past successes in avoiding capture had emboldened them enough to throw caution to the wind. Now they were taking unnecessary chances.

Chapter Twenty-six

An Eye for an Eye

The clans living back in the hidden coves seldom received outsiders well. Most remained secretive, suspicious and often dangerous to those foolish enough to trespass on their domains. Only members of their kindred could enter their stomping grounds with impunity and John Graham Hiram and I were far from being kinfolks. For us to gain access and garner the least suspicion we needed to perpetuate a good ruse. Being the sheriff, Hiram was universally well-known and easily recognized throughout the county and he realized that someone other than himself would be needed to go into hostile territory in search of the Tishams.

I was puzzled when one day he sent word that I should meet him in his home instead of the usual place of the sheriff's office. I thought "This odd."

I had been invited into his home knowing he liked to keep his private life private. When I arrived there, Mrs. Hiram greeted me at the door and invited me in. She said the sheriff had stepped out but would return shortly. I entered and was promptly introduced to an uncle of the sheriff who was also waiting. We exchanged pleasantries and I seated myself on the couch while his uncle sat in an adjoining chair.

He was a distinguished-looking gentleman, slightly overweight, well-groomed, and with a bushy, grey beard. I was slightly uncomfortable in the company of this stranger and struggled to think of an interesting subject of conservation. As a result, we remained quiet and waited patiently for the sheriff to return. I finally managed to ask if he was visiting our area or lived nearby. He responded that he was only visiting and lived over near Centerville. After that, we sat quietly again and waited.

After a few minutes, we were joined again by Mrs. Hiram who asked, "How are you two getting along?"

"Fine ma'am, we are doing fine. Just waiting for the sheriff to return."

Imagine my surprise when Mrs. Hiram laughed and said, "Well, John, I guess your disguise will work."

With that revelation, the sheriff stood and removed a pad from his midriff and the beard from his face. He smiled content that I had not recognized him. I knew he would go to any length to find and capture the infamous Tishams, but never realized his talent for deception. I had been thoroughly fooled by his theatrics. His wife laughed and explained that, when in school John had excelled in drama classes. He often got the leading roles in plays, but any aspirations he had had for the theater were abandoned for his greater love of law enforcement. I had no idea of the extent of his talents, and he soon proved to be a true master of deception.

Sheriff Hiram had devised a plan that would enable us to travel those hostile backroads with impunity. He would pretend to be a purchasing agent for the railroad, and I would serve as his guide. Our charade was that we were looking to buy timber for crossties. The sheriff even had business cards printed to present to unsuspecting landowners which made us appear legitimate and professional. Most of the people we approached would listen to our proposal if they thought there was a potential for money to be made.

Uncle Tabor loaned us an old truck and Sheriff Hiram had a local sign painter paint in bold letters "Timber Purchasing & Logging Co." across both doors. He then donned his bushy beard, and we drove most of the backroads without raising suspicion so our theatrics proved successful. Sheriff Hiram traveled without displaying his badge, so we drove the roads incognito. We were satisfied with our deception and the fact that no one recognized us or suspected our purpose. Still, we were not necessarily welcomed in the "stomping ground" of all we met, and that gave us a reason for suspicion. Were they hiding something? Any areas where we were denied access were areas we suspected the Tishams could be hiding.

I couldn't help but feel guilty knowing that when the Tishams were captured, their pipe dream of an easy source of cash would evaporate like the early morning mist. Sheriff Hiram reminded me that there would be a reward for the person giving information leading to the capture of the moonshiners. Also, if a tract proved promising, then it could possibly be bought and harvested by the railroad or my father for his sawmill. That lessened my concern only slightly.

When approaching a house, we were usually greeted first by a pack of barking hounds then a person brandishing a rifle or shotgun would emerge from inside and gruffly ask us what our business was there. We tried to remain professional and politely introduced ourselves while handing them one of our business cards and telling them we were looking to buy timber for the Great Southern Railroad. Once the occupants heard there was the possibility of money for timber they usually relaxed and asked for more details.

Sheriff Hiram would then go into a canned speech saying that we were looking to purchase tracts of timber provided there would be no objections from family members or neighbors that may resent us traipsing over their property to evaluate the timber. We then weighed each reaction for vague clues like, "Uncle Joe doesn't like people poking around up there." We were quick to follow up with, "No problem, we understand but please keep us in mind."

We didn't want to appear overly anxious. A check mark was then placed by the area we didn't need to be poking around in and of course that would be an area of suspicion.

Sheriff Hiram and I traveled backroads that I never knew existed. Others I had been aware of but had never had a reason to travel. Some were so overgrown and unkempt that they reminded me of the old Scenic I had traveled many years earlier when planning my visit with Gerty Goforth. Limbs and vines hung so heavy over one road that I often had to exit our truck and lift branches or other debris from our path. It was good that we were driving Uncle Tabor's old farm truck because all the dents and scratches we added would go unnoticed.

John Graham Hiram was more determined than ever to find Doyle and Doolittle Tisham and bring them to justice. He was willing to drive every road and pig trail on the mountain if necessary. While driving up one road, which was little more than a cow path, we came upon a fallen tree blocking our progress. Sheriff Hiram pulled our truck to the side, parked and removed an axe he always carried to cut up stills but was now needed to remove the obstacle. As we approached the tree, we noticed that it had been deliberately felled evidently to block or slow any traveler's passage.

"Well," he said, "It appears that someone doesn't want visitors on this ridge."

"That's a dead giveaway. We must be getting close," I said.

The sheriff began cutting, and I removed the brush and tossed it over the mountainside into a deep ravine that skirted our passage.

"Listen," he said, "I hear a car approaching; someone's coming."

Sheriff Hiram quickly placed his axe back in the bed of the truck, straightened his fake beard and removed a rifle from the truck. He asked me to step behind the truck and stay low in case it was the Tishams. We were surprised when old Marmaduke MacKurdy appeared; his truck piled high with wood. He pulled behind our truck and sat with his motor running, never offering to help us remove the obstacle. We noticed he was also hauling a large wooden crate containing a very agitated razorback hog.

"Gracious," the sheriff said, "What in the world are you doing hauling around a wild hog?"

"Traded for it. An old woman down the road couldn't pay cash after I unloaded her wood, so I traded for the hog instead. Don't need it, but I ain't giving away free wood either. You need a hog?" he asked the sheriff.

"Lordy, no!" he answered, "I have an old sow with eight or ten piglets back home. I don't need another right now."

As Marmaduke became comfortable, he exited his truck and stood with his hands tucked under the bibb of his overalls.

"You're Marmaduke MacKurdy, aren't you?" the sheriff asked, pretending not to be familiar with him. Leaning toward the ground, Marmaduke spit a wad of juice from a chew of tobacco bulging inside his jaw.

Looking back over his shoulder and up and down the road he answered, "Yeah, I'm Marmaduke. How do you know me?"

"I don't rightly know you, Mr. MacKurdy, but I have heard of you and of your blessings of delivering firewood to all the poor widows up and down the mountain."

"Everybody knows you, Marmaduke. You're famous in these parts," I added.

Marmaduke straightened, took on a proud posture and boastfully answered, "Yeah, I guess most folks around these parts know me. From delivering wood, I mean."

"Where are you headed now, Marmaduke?" the sheriff asked.

"Got wood deliveries to make. Customers waiting." Marmaduke answered nervously.

Delivering firewood, I thought, remembering the time we loaded his hidden compartments with moonshine. I was fairly sure he was delivering more than firewood. Firewater maybe!

"It looks as if someone doesn't want visitors nosing around up here. Someone deliberately felled this tree," the sheriff said. "We will have it removed shortly."

Marmaduke never suspected it was the sheriff addressing him, and there was no sign that he recognized me.

"I guess a fellow needs to be careful poking around up here," Marmaduke replied nervously.

"Well, our business is buying timber. Nothing more." The sheriff offered.

The sheriff looked at me, grinned, and then, looking at Marmaduke, added, "I guess neither of us has anything to worry about, then, do we?"

"I ain't worried," protested Marmaduke. Not worried at all. It's just that I have heard rumors. So y,all be careful." He seemed to become more agitated at that point and then abruptly said. "I was just over on Fancher's Ridge delivering wood, you know, and was told that it would probably be best to stay out of Hawkins Hollow. I've heard told that there are some mean characters up there."

Now the sheriff had a reason for concern. "Mean characters? You think someone up there would harm two innocent timber purchasers?"

Marmaduke realized he had said too much and quickly added, "Please don't say anything. I can't have anyone knowing I told you this cause them boys can be mighty dangerous I've been told. Some misfits making bad whiskey. They need to be stopped before someone gets hurt."

Sheriff Hiram nodded in agreement, winked shyly at me and replied, "Great, Marmaduke, we need more good, honest citizens like you, but whoever is up here is no concern of ours. We are just looking to buy timber. We'll say nothing of your intelligence and consider your name is as good as forgotten, but I strongly suggest you heed those warnings and stay out of Hawkins Hollow as well."

The sheriff now wore an expression of concern as he turned to finish removing the last of the obstacle on the ground. Marmaduke said nothing more as he returned to his truck, drove around us, and continued toward the forbidden hollow. He completely ignored the warning. I said nothing of what I thought Marmaduke's real purpose was for being here on the mountain but suspected the sheriff knew more than he was letting on.

"What was all that about?" I asked, a little confused with the sheriff's conversation.

"I was planting seeds," he answered. "Giving him something to think about. You are probably not aware that he is delivering more than firewood. I have long known that delivering wood is a cover while he is carrying on a well-established sideline of delivering moonshine."

I was shocked by the sheriff's revelation and asked, "If you know he is a bootlegger, why haven't we arrested the old codger?"

"It's a matter of priorities," he answered. "As long as people drink whiskey there will be bootleggers. When old Wash Tisham first came to the mountain people said that his whiskey was some of the best made. Unfortunately, his boys are not concerned with quality or safety, only about the money they can make. Their product has proven to be harmful and borders on poisonous. Marmaduke's source of moonshine has proven to be good-tasting whiskey made the old-fashioned way and is safer to drink. That is the reason I haven't arrested him. When given a choice, I would rather my friends who drink have a choice of buying their whiskey from Marmaduke than the rotgut from the Tishams. Once we eliminate the Tishams then we will turn our attention to Marmaduke and put him out of business as well.

I couldn't help but be reminded of my brief involvement with moonshining a few years back when helping Otis and my uncles down in Oral Hollow. Thankfully, those days are long forgotten, otherwise, it might be me Sheriff Hiram was looking for.

Marmaduke disappeared around the curve and we soon followed. From the road we drove we entered a few side roads and carefully checked each for clues. None showed evidence of our quarry, so we returned to the main road and continued driving into the mountain. Then we noticed a side road that crossed a deep gulley through a covered bridge. In the distance, at the foot of a steep ridge, we could see a large barn, and our attention was drawn to columns of smoke rising from both open hallways.

"Looks like someone is drying tobacco," I observed.

The sheriff slid to a stop!

"That is kind of odd. We passed fields with evidence of corn but nothing indicating tobacco. I think we may have found what we have been looking for."

We found a place to turn our truck around and drove back to the covered bridge as discreetly as possible. The bridge was barricaded at its entrance and had a crudely written sign warning trespassers to "Keep Out, all will be shot!" The sheriff removed a spyglass and carefully scanned the area around the distant barn.

"I see several dogs lying out front and an old car backed into the hallway but no people," the sheriff reported. "I am sure they are there, just don't see them. Those hounds will be a problem. There is no way to approach without them warning the occupants."

It was then that he hesitated and said, "Wait, I see Doolittle. He is putting something into the trunk of an automobile. Thank goodness, we have found our culprits at last."

We hurried off the mountain and discussed how to best approach our quarry without alerting the dogs.

"I think I may have a solution," Sheriff Hiram announced.

It wasn't long until our descent was obscured by a trail of dust as we fell in behind the stubborn old bootlegger Marmaduke. He had deliberately ignored our warnings. At our first opportunity, the sheriff gunned our truck, roared around Marmaduke, and continued down the mountain.

"He obviously doesn't understand or believe he is in danger by coming up here," The sheriff said.

The sheriff and I returned to Trickum, where he removed his false beard and padded waistband and called for the assembly of his deputies. When all had gathered, I counted nine excluding the head lawman and myself. Sheriff Hiram insisted on keeping the details of our discovery secret. He didn't want to give anyone sympathetic to the Tishams any chance of warning them.

"We need a way to get rid of those hounds, or they will warn the boys of our approach, but I think I may have a solution for that problem."

The sheriff asked the deputies to meet at the jail at five a.m. to have time for coffee and organize our equipment. By six, everyone had arrived, and all were understandably anxious to begin our raid. We were all surprised when Sheriff Hiram arrived hauling the wooden crate containing Marmaduke's wild hog. Dumbfounded, they asked why he had the pig and whether he was planning to have a bar be que? He only smiled and said to wait, and we would understand.

We were puzzled but we loaded our vehicles and headed off for Hawkins Hollow hauling that hog. After a forty-five-minute drive, we stopped short of the bridge that crossed over to the "tobacco barn" and suspected moonshine still. The eastern sky was now starting to

BRIDGE WHERE SHERIFF HIRAM PUT HOG OUT

lighten enough to work without the need of lanterns. We were still dumbfounded as to the reason for bringing a pig to a raid.

Looking through his telescope, the sheriff could see signs of activity at the barn. A lantern inside the hallway cast thin strips of light through the cracks in the boarded walls. A dog yelped, possibly from being stepped on or kicked from underfoot. The sheriff asks us to unload his hog as quietly as possible and place it at the far end of the bridge. He asked us to wait until he gave a signal and then release the hog. Looking at each other and shaking our heads, we agreed to release it on his command.

"I'll let out a loud squeal like an animal in distress and then you quickly release the porker," he directed. That will alert their dogs, which I expect will come running, and, seeing a fleeing hog, will turn and pursue it up that ridge."

With that, he let out a blood-curdling squeal, and the dogs ran barking toward the bridge at full speed.

"Now, release her!"

We opened the cage and out roared a highly agitated porker. Seeing a wild boar charging toward them confused the dogs at first, and they scattered, but then they turned and instinctively chased after it as it ran through the barn lot and up the mountainside. Hearing the sudden uproar of the dogs, the moonshiners, expecting trouble rushed from the barn with guns raised and ready for a fight. Then, seeing the dogs chasing the hog, they realized what had caused the commotion, and they lowered their weapons and began cheering for their favorite hound. They had been completely fooled and were unaware that the sheriff and the deputies were closing in.

Doyle, Doolittle, and their gang stood amused at the sounds of the chase and were totally unaware of the danger approaching through a thin morning mist. There was laughter and cheering as each bet on the dog he thought would tree first. Suddenly, the posse appeared from the shadows and rushed forward.

"Boys," the sheriff called out loudly, "Surrender now or be annihilated."

The Tishams had no intention of giving up and, as always, were geared for a fight. They turned and fled back into the protection of the barn while shouting obscenities toward the deputies. Straight away, sharp reports of gunfire reverberated up and down the mountainside. It brought to mind the amplified cracking of tinder being tossed onto a heaping pile of bone-dry brush. Instead of hanging back, as I had in earlier engagements, I charged forward, energized by thoughts of my little brother June Bug. I feared neither for life nor limb. I was filled with anger and desperately wanted revenge for my little brother.

It is hard to describe the sound of a bullet as it zips past your head. There is a sharp cracking, similar to the snap of a whip, followed a split second later by the report of the distant gun. They say you never hear the shot that kills you. I understand now, after so much frustration you simply harden yourself to the possibility of death and you ignore it. You are finally able to accept whatever God has planned for you and you go for it.

I found myself numbed to the realities surrounding me, and I rushed into the battle braver than I had ever been. I could hear the thuds of missiles striking boards and bones and the painful cries of anguish. I was oblivious to the pandemonium surrounding me but saddened by the cries of pain and dying. Brother Doyle was the first to fall, possibly from my own bullet. I wanted desperately to punish the Tishams for all their treachery and for hurting my little brother. As his final breaths were drawn, Doyle lay sprawled in the rotted hay and cow manure, and his blue eyes searched in vain for his little brother Doolittle.

Doolittle continued to fight with a devilish ferocity. He fired his weapon with wild abandon, all the while yelling insults and promising to avenge his brother's wounds.

I was no longer intimidated by his threats. I had become immune. I was now a veteran of battle, hardened by the memories of the infamous gunfight years earlier when they killed the poor deputies and by the tragic lynching of the prisoner John Mulley for Doolittle's crimes and finally, I was agonized by the image of my little brother lying dead in our family parlor.

Doolittle called out threats of vengeance for his brother's killing. Just as it happened back at the Tishams years ago, the barn quickly filled with a cloud of thick, blinding smoke from all the shooting. Again, men were firing aimlessly at sounds instead of at adversaries. Then, a new horror occurred. Whether it was from the firing of the guns into dry hay or an overturned lantern, a fire broke out and the barn quickly became engulfed in flames. I knew men were going to be burned without mercy.

A couple were apprehended as they ran from the flames. A couple were shot but their wounds were only minor and they would survive. As mean as he was, Doyle died before being consumed in the fire. He had mercifully avoided a preview of hell. His charred body was recovered with his hands still grasping his gun. The fate of Doolittle, however, remained unknown; his body was not discovered. He had managed once again to slip past the posse by taking advantage of the thick screen of smoke. Three bootleggers, counting Doyle, had perished, and with the exception of Doolittle, the others had been captured. Only two deputies had been wounded and those only slightly. The sheriff counted his blessings. Unfortunately, Doolittle had again taken on the persona of a folk hero. He truly seemed invincible, but John Graham Hiram was not discouraged; he was still as determined as ever to bring his old adversary to justice. Now, at least, he had reduced the gang to one final antagonist and remained steadfast in his quest to bring him down.

Chapter Twenty-seven

Marmaduke's Farewell

The sheriff became alarmed when citizens from different locations around the county expressed concerns that Marmaduke had not been seen for several days. He had failed to make his "wood" deliveries as expected and people were becoming worried. The Sheriff was worried too. He remembered that Marmaduke had ignored his warnings and continued to make deliveries into areas thought to have been locations used by the Tisham gang. The sheriff asked his deputies to keep their eyes and ears open for any clues to Marmaduke's whereabouts.

John Graham Hiram and I were once again driving the Scenic and discussing the puzzling disappearance of Marmaduke. He and his truck had vanished into thin air. But then, as we passed above the old Tisham homeplace a glint of light caught our attention. Something was out of place down there. The sheriff stopped his truck, and we cautiously descended the hillside and approached the abandoned house. To our surprise and concern, we discovered that the glint of light that had alarmed us was reflected from the windshield of Marmaduke's truck. It had been partially hidden under a cover of broken pine limbs. A quick check inside revealed a seat stained with blood but nothing of Marmaduke. As we approached the house we could hear weak and muffled pleas for help coming from inside. With our guns drawn we entered the home and found poor Marmaduke there but barely alive. He had been beaten severely and obviously left for dead. He was bound to a chair in the middle of the very room where I had seen the infamous gunfight years earlier. He managed to confirm that his tormentor had been Doolittle Tisham.

Barely able to speak, he told us that Doolittle had accused him of ratting out the location of their last moonshine operation, which led to the gang's ultimate destruction. Doolittle promised to kill him as slowly and as painfully as possible.

"Where is he now?" the sheriff asked.

"I don't know, He hasn't been here since yesterday. Please, get me to a doctor," Marmaduke begged in barely a whisper.

The sheriff instructed me to bring our truck down the hill so we could load Marmaduke and rush him to the doctor as quickly as possible. Poor, pitiful Marmaduke was barely hanging on. We found a few remaining bits of ragged mattresses which we removed from the shanty, placed them in the bed of the truck and loaded Marmaduke on them to help cushion his ride. With me cradling his bloody head in my lap we sped off toward the doctor's office and Trickum. Marmaduke moaned in pain each time we bounced over a bump or fell into a rut. Finally arriving at the doctor's office, we carried Marmaduke inside.

The Sheriff and I waited while the doctor worked as best as he could to save him. Then after nearly an hour, the doctor came to tell us that unfortunately Marmaduke didn't survive. The old legend was gone.

The county would have two funerals now. I thought it doubtful if either would be well attended. Marmaduke was expected to have a few members of his family in attendance. His service was held on Big Grove Mountain and surprisingly at the same little church where I had disappointed my Grandmother Blackspaniel years ago. Sheriff John Graham Hiram and I attended his funeral and stood just inside the door with our hats in our hands. I casually glanced around and was shocked to see none other than Willow Countess and her mother in attendance. They were dressed in black and standing with the family of MacKurdy.

Approaching her I asked, "Hello Willow, I am surprised to see you here. Did you know Mr. MacKurdy?"

Willow responded, "Yes. You had no way of knowing, but Mother and Marmaduke were first cousins."

I was almost speechless. It truly is a small world. I was also surprised that Willow had regained some of her former radiance. She now appeared more vibrant and her beautiful smile seemed to be returning.

When I inquired what had been the cause of her improvement she said, "You! You returned to my life and that is the reason."

"But what about the days I have been away lately and haven't been able to see you?"

"Do you mean the time it took for you to finally settle the score with the Tishams? Your old friend Pinkney has kept me informed. He shared the news from your local newspaper, the Trickum Whispers. Thank God it is finally finished and you can find closure."

Sheriff Hiram and I attended the services for Doyle Tisham as well. I think the sheriff wanted to pay his respects and I went because I wanted to be sure he was dead. He was laid to rest next to his parents in the cemetery at Five Corners Methodist Church. Neither the pastor nor the congregation would allow his service to be held inside the church for fear the devil himself might be in attendance. I doubted that, thinking the devil was probably too busy poking Doyle with his pitchfork somewhere other than the church.

The sheriff, remembering that Doyle and Dolittle had been inseparable during their life figured that Doolittle might find it impossible to resist attending his brother's funeral. He placed a couple of deputies on the outskirts of the cemetery to watch for him in case he tried to attend. Brother Edgar was still incarcerated somewhere up in Tennessee and their nieces Milly and Molly were the only family that felt an obligation to attend their uncle Doyle's funeral. A compassionate Sheriff, Hiram, was kind enough to provide for their transportation from Big Grove Mountain. The funeral director, the sheriff, and I were the only other folks to pay our respects at Doyle's burial. I certainly did not respect him, but I did feel sympathy for his nieces. If Doolittle watched from the shadows, he was discreet and we never saw him.

Chapter Twenty-eight
Doolittle's Demise

An early morning mist lay heavy over the swollen banks of Bear Creek. A freshet after midnight had flooded the hollow and Aunt Minnie found it necessary to speak to her children in raised tones to be heard above the roar of churning water. But as the sun's rays warmed and burned off the vapor the form of a vehicle appeared half submerged just below the crossing at what is normally a shallow ford. Aunt Fannie called her oldest son to go quickly and investigate. After walking partway to the creek with him, she turned and noticed the figure of a man disappearing around the curve at the top of the hill. Her son reported that the truck door was opened, but no one remained inside. Aunt Fannie wondered why anyone would try to drive their vehicle through the flooded torrent and then abandon their automobile.

She instructed her son to saddle their mule and ride to Five Corners and find help. It took just a little more than two hours for him to ride up the northern bank of the creek and across two smaller tributaries before finding a crossing shallow enough for his mule to wade over to the south side. By the time we all arrived back at the creek, the water had drained sufficiently for us to be able to wade in and examine the half-submerged truck. I immediately recognized the vehicle as belonging to the late Marmaduke MacKurdy. Its last known location was back at the old Tisham residence with two flat tires. The high side boards had been removed making the truck less recognizable. While we scoured the banks for casualties, Aunt Minnie informed us of the lone figure of the man she had seen disappearing over the crest of the hill. A few minutes later, the sheriff arrived and confirmed that the truck being washed in the creek was indeed Marmaduke's, and he was sure the driver had been none other than Doolittle Tisham.

We immediately set out climbing the steep hill in the direction of the fleeing suspect. At the top of the hill, we hesitated long enough to catch our breaths and heard calls for help from the direction of Mr. McDuffy's mine. Climbing down we found Mr. Mc Duffy distraught and with blood streaming from his forehead.

"What happened, John?" the sheriff asked.

"I was attacked by Doolittle Tisham," he responded. "Struck me with one of my own shovels."

"Where did he go? Where is he now?" the sheriff asked.

"He ran into the mine there!" John replied while pointing into the dark entrance of the tunnel. "He shouldn't have gone in there. I was out here to fetch timbers to shore up a weak place in the roof. It is near collapsing."

"Is there another way out?" the sheriff asked.

"No, this is it!"

Looking toward me, the sheriff said, "Well, Daniel, it looks like we have finally cornered our man. Now we just have to figure out how to best smoke him out."

I wanted to end the drama as much as anyone but didn't want to enter that darkened cavern without plenty of protection and light.

"How should we proceed?" I asked.

"Well," the sheriff answered, "We started with dogs; let us finish with dogs."

With that, he sent me off to fetch our faithful hounds. Being smaller and able to see in the dark made them far superior to us larger targets.

Doolittle had received a good soaking when trying to ford the creek at flood stage. Abandoning the vehicle mid-stream he had barely managed to pull himself to shore with the aid of branches that extended into the stream. Now, he huddled in the dark recesses of the McDuffy mine, fearing a rush of vigilantes trying to arrest him. Being alone in the dark for a period of time causes one's imagination to conjure up all kinds of scenarios. Poor, shivering Doolittle surely imagined hearing the phantom whispers and faint footsteps of approaching vigilantes. Striking the flint of a carbide lamp, he grabbed when entering the mine, he held it aloft and searched the recesses for any deeper void in which to hide. The sheriff called often and loudly for his surrender. His calls were surely heard as they echoed down the shaft, but if Doolittle heard his pleas he did not respond. Finally, the dogs were brought to the entrance and strained at their leashes as the posse entered the mine.

Mr. McDuffy repeatedly warned us of the danger of entering the mine until he could shore up the unstable part of the ceiling about which he was so concerned.

"I am sorry John," the sheriff responded. "We've waited too long to back off now."

We entered the shaft with caution, and hesitated at every corner, allowing our dogs to sniff out our quarry. Deeper and deeper we went and always with our guns raised. As we crept along I was aware that coal mines were far more dangerous than the caverns I had explored in my youth. The mines were recently dug by man while caves were thousands of years old and made by God. I trusted God's work to be far more stable. I whispered another prayer as we continued our dangerous search.

The hounds continued to pull us deeper into the mine, and their barking echoed through the blackness. The sheriff repeated his calls for Doolittle to surrender but received no response. Finally, we approached the latest of John McDuffy's digs where we found it necessary to crouch to avoid the low ceiling. The dogs were now snapping at the heels of a desperate and determined Doolittle Tisham as he pushed behind a beam Mr. McDuffy had placed temporarily to support the unstable roof of the mine.

As he struggled to avoid capture, Doolittle shoved the beam to the side and at first only a few small rocks and dust fell but remembering Mr. McDuffey's warning, the sheriff knew the whole mountain was about to cave in.

Sheriff Hiram called out, "Run Daniel, it's coming down."

We turned and fled at full speed. I had not run so fast since that day back in the Bear Creek Gulch when trying to escape the dreaded White Thang. Our dogs turned and skedaddled even faster. It is a wonder that the wind didn't extinguish the flames of our lanterns. A low rumble and then a deafening crash, growing in intensity, signaled that the mine was collapsing behind us. All we heard from the doomed Doolittle Tisham was a muffled cry. We were fleeing at full speed when we were suddenly expelled from the mine entrance by a blast of dust and debris. Doolittle, unfortunately, had chosen to be entombed forever under the weight of Grace Mountain. At long last the infamous Tisham gang was no more.

Chapter Twenty-nine

A Time for Angels

Oddly, after the dust had settled, no one rejoiced. There was no cheering. I was satisfied that justice had been served and another guilty man had been punished, but Mr. McDuffey's mine had collapsed and we all regretted that. In the days that followed, things returned to normal, and I turned my attention to winning the heart of my angel. I refused to wait another minute. The week following Doolittle's last hoorah, I arrived at Angel's Switch with all the confidence any person could muster. I hurried to the Countess' residence, knocked at the door, and shortly after it opened, there stood Willow. My heart soared. She was still frail but on the mend and again wearing that beautiful smile that I first fell in love with.

"Please, come in Daniel," she said backing away from the entrance.

Sitting in the center of the living room was a bright-eyed toddler about two years old. He was clearly the image of his mother who had first captured my heart.

"Daniel, this is my little Robby. Robby, this is my friend Daniel. Can you say, 'Hi'?"

Robby looked up at me, smiled, and said, "Hello, Mr. Daniel" and then he returned to the toy he was playing with.

"He's beautiful," I said, "You must be proud of him."

I will have to admit, I was jealous that he wasn't mine. But I realized that it was no fault of this precious little angel who stared up through those deep blue eyes.

"Daniel, can you ever forgive me? I feel like such a fool. I never intended for things to happen the way they did. When I never heard from you, I thought you had forgotten me. And when they found your letters, I was devastated, but then it was too late. I was sure I had lost you forever."

I had so many emotions running through my head. I was overjoyed that I finally had a chance of winning Willow's love and hopefully the trust of her mother. I knew that I could love little Robby without hesitation, and I could raise him as my child. Life for me now held promise and within weeks I asked Willow to marry me. She accepted, and believe it or not with her mother's blessing.

Our wedding was performed in the Angel's Switch Fellowship Church by their new pastor. My old friend Pinkney served as my best man and little Robby as our ring bearer. One of my greatest joys was when the preacher said, "I now pronounce you husband and wife. You may kiss the bride."

I have not had the pleasure of experiencing many kisses, but I'll never forget that one, the most tender, memorable, and exciting event of my life.

Willow and I set up housekeeping in Angel's Switch, and I became a partner with Pinkney at his construction company. We mainly contract to build homes, and we are both reasonably successful. Life is good here, but I will never forget growing up on Grace Mountain. I will always cherish my memories from there, remembering that even with the ugliness of the likes of the Tishams, goodness eventually wins, and life goes on. We were the underprivileged and the downtrodden, but we never ever gave up.

The end

Ken Pennington ©2024